Problems in American Civilization

Individualism
and Conformity
in the AMERICAN
CHARACTER

EDITED WITH AN INTRODUCTION BY

Richard L. Rapson

UNIVERSITY OF HAWAII

D. C. HEATH AND COMPANY
A Division of Raytheon Education Company
Lexington, Massachusetts

INTRODUCTION

AMERICANS have always craved self-definition. In fact, one of the chief justifications for the study of an exclusively *American* history rests on the assumption that Americans are different from the citizens of other nations. Such an assumption cannot be proven, but only a small number of scholars and average men question it very seriously. On the contrary, the American traveler on his way home from a trip to Europe or Asia, while recognizing qualities which are universal to all human beings, generally returns with a new sense of the ways in which Americans vary from the people among whom he has recently been visiting.

There has consequently been a persistent and irresistible effort on the part of all who would write about America to discover the key which might unlock the door to the American character. What is an American? What are his traits? How did he get to be the way he is? How does he differ from a Frenchman? from a Russian? from an Englishman? from a Chinese? Has the American character changed through time?

The answers to these questions have exhausted nearly every possibility; some have been illuminating, too many have been fanciful. Yet a strange sort of order underlies the apparent chaos. David Potter, one of the most perceptive students of the American character, has noted that despite the infinite possibilities opened up by these queries, "it is probably safe to say that at bottom there have been only two primary ways of explaining the American, and that almost all of the innumerable interpretations which have been formulated can be grouped around or at least oriented to these two basic explanations . . ."[1]

The surprising element in this finding is that the "two primary ways of explaining the American" appear to stand in direct contradiction of one another for "one depicts the American primarily as an individualist and an idealist, while the other makes him out as a conformist and materialist."[2] The readings in this volume undertake to recreate this continuing debate and to place the student in a position to line up along one of the two poles or else determine whether and under what conditions the two positions are reconcilable.

But before turning to these substantive issues, several methodological questions must be asked. Can we assume that there is such a thing as national character? What exactly is meant by the phrase? Where does one look to find this character? To behavior? institutions? history? values? environment? psyche? What molds it? How completely do a culture's "traits" condition the life of the individual member of the culture? Under what circumstances, if any, can a national character be altered?

Merely to ask these questions makes it immediately clear that neither the meaning nor the existence of national character is self-evident. While it is not within the scope of this introduction to settle these issues,[3] a few points may be made.

[1] David M. Potter, "The Quest for the National Character," in John Higham, ed., *The Reconstruction of American History* (New York: Harper & Row, 1962), p. 198.

[2] *Ibid.*, p. 198.

[3] The reader is referred to the bibliography at the end of this book.

First, historians as well as American and foreign travelers have often debased the concept of national character. Methodological questions have been faced only on rare occasions. Stockpiles of national stereotypes have been accumulated and have served to heighten national jingoism and the distrust of others. Portraits of national groups have been sloppy, imprecise, and inconsistent.

Second, loose and ambiguous generalization about national groups should not disqualify the concept of national character from serious historical analysis. Because "national character" is a conceptual model and not a tangible reality, the user of the model must create definitions, make clear his criteria and try to follow them as consistently as possible.

Third, a major step toward clarity may be made by distinguishing among the various kinds of traits which may be attributed to a culture. Potter writes:

Very often a catalogue of traits ranges from the profound to the trivial. Thus we may be told in the same breath that Americans are optimistic (a trait of temperament), that they attach great value to productive activity (a trait of character), that they are fond of jazz music (a cultural trait), and that they are remarkably prone to join organized groups (a behavioral trait which may provide overt evidence of some underlying trait of character). In the discussion of national character it probably would not be either practicable or rewarding to enforce these distinctions rigidly, but analysis of the subject would not be quite so loose as it is if writers had at least recognized that traits of character are at one level and distinctive habits, such as addiction to some particular articles of diet, are at quite another.[4]

If the reader can make these distinctions, he will already be far ahead of most of those who have drawn prose portraits of the American character. He will be in a better position to identify those traits of character and culture which are connected with deeply entrenched values.

In the following essays the reader will come upon examples of rigor as well as instances of inexcusable carelessness as various qualities are attributed to Americans. Although our major interest here is with the web of relationships which compose the American character, the student who demands and looks for precision and definition from his authors will find himself far better equipped to tackle the larger questions involved in the attempt to characterize what Americans are like. When an observer describes a trait of Americans, the reader should ask himself: "Is this a superficial behavioral quality or does it tie in with deeper assumptions about life — assumptions which may be peculiar to Americans?"

The first section of this collection deals with an observer who consciously attempted to explore the depths of the American character as it was shaped by a democratic culture. Alexis de Tocqueville's analysis still stands as the monument to which all subsequent studies have paid and continue to pay homage. He did not choose between individualism and conformity when he wrote of the American. He noted the prevalence of both qualities. The greatness of his achievement may be found in his effort to construct a model of the American character which holds them both together in a paradoxical relationship. The first two selections from *Democracy in America* trace individualism and then conformity to their sources, while the

[4] David M. Potter, *People of Plenty: Economic Abundance and the American Character* (Chicago: Univ. of Chicago, 1954), p. 12.

third reflects his effort to place them both within a larger conceptual framework.

After beginning with Tocqueville's complex model, this volume then works backward and forward along two tracks. Part Two includes five selections from commentators who stressed the individualistic aspects of the American character. Part Three is composed of three essays by those who saw Americans chiefly as conformists. With the exception of the pieces by Jefferson and Turner, the first eleven selections come from the pens of foreign observers. The perspective of a foreign observer is particularly valuable because the inhabitant of a culture tends to take the essential institutions and values of his own culture for granted. The outsider automatically compares American culture with his own, and when he notes large differences he concentrates on them.

In the second and third sections an attempt is made also to trace individualism and conformity back to their roots. Certain themes repeat themselves in the former case. The writers connect individualism with the newness of the historical experience or with agriculture or with the west or with the frontier. But since the historical experience is no longer new, since industry dominates agriculture in the twentieth century, since the frontier has become settled and urbanized, one naturally wonders whether Americans who might once have been individualists may not now live in an environment which nurtures interdependence, not self-reliance. David Riesman, in the opening essay of Part Four, writes of an American character which has changed from a confident individualism in the nineteenth century to an anxious conformity in the twentieth. The change from an agrarian rural

order to an industrial, urban society, if it has affected the national character, poses serious questions of value as well. Is the change creating a one-dimensional man in a mass society, or is it forging a new equilibrium of individualism and conformity?

The final portion of this collection, then, pivots on the question of a changing national character and the validity of the assumption that there has been a change in the basic values of our culture. Riesman's hypothesis has been attacked from two quarters: first, from those who contend that nineteenth-century Americans were not, in fact, individualists; and second, from those who deny that twentieth-century Americans are conformists. The last four essays do more, however, than simply question Riesman's popular view. Each proposes a new way of talking about the American; each calls for original and more complex approaches. Each calls for new questions, new postulations, for precision and subtlety in the analysis of the American character. The essays by Bell, Potter, and Lipset are especially sophisticated, and every serious student of American history needs to ponder the importance of the contributions of these three scholars. With the exception of a small excision from the Lipset article, these three essays are reproduced in their entirety so that the reader may share the author's full complexity of thought and thus be invited to respond to them with his own best thoughts.

The individualist-conformist controversy has assumed several different shapes. The American has been seen either as an individualist or as a conformist. He has been seen changing from being an individualist toward becoming a conformist. In a position which calls for new terminology, he has been seen as an amalgam of the two poles or in a state of tension between them. The question is a crucial one for the historian because the position he takes concerning the relationship between individualism and conformity in the American character tends to control his view of political and social conflict in American history.

Throughout most of this century, until the outbreak of World War II, the dominant interpretation of the American past suggested the presence of *two* national characters locked in permanent, constant conflict. It depicted a society deeply divided by the conflict between conservatives and liberals, between businessmen and poor people, between materialists and idealists. This view is most closely associated with the names of Charles Beard, Carl Becker, Louis Hacker, both Arthur Schlesingers — Senior and Junior, V. L. Parrington, and, to some extent, Frederick Jackson Turner. In their spirited and influential writings they portrayed a nation in dramatic, unceasing conflict, with one side dominant and then the other. Arthur Schlesinger, Sr. even calculated the average span of years during which conservative or liberal would be ascendant in the pendulum of American history.

Today we live in a period of apparent consensus, a period when bitter class, economic, and ideological struggles appear to be muted. Hence, during the last two decades, in the reinterpretation of the American past, the similarities between contesting groups have been emphasized; old and epic debates have been seen as shadow-bouts; our common assumptions have been rated far more significant than the "illusory" differences. This "cult of consensus," as John Higham has called it, can be seen in the final portion of this book, most clearly in Lipset's essay as he labors to reconcile the two extremes around which the controversy over the American character has raged. Just as we are now told that we are all Federalists and all Republicans, as we are all Lockeans and all entrepreneurs, so too we are now all individualists and all conformists — and always have been.

The analysts of consensus may be right, but one cannot help wondering whether the contemporary view may not be too present-minded; whether a future depression or a division in society, should either ever occur, may not make us seriously reconsider the older view which now has been largely discredited. The historians of conflict, unfortunately, wrote chiefly of movements in American history rather than directly of the American character. Only implicitly can we link up the American as individualist with their celebration of the liberal idealists of the past, or the American as conformist with their derogation of the conservative materialists. No single writing of this group of scholars explicitly carries out their conception of American history into a direct statement on the simultaneous existence of two American characters; but it is an implied position which should not be overlooked.

When the reader asks himself whether individualism or conformity dominates the American character, whether that character has altered, whether that change has affected the patterns of political and social conflict, whether one can join together or keep in tension these two polar positions, or whether altogether different terminology may be better suited to this entire discussion, he is asking one of the more important questions in the study of American history. But he is doing much more than that: he is asking a significant question about himself as well.

CONTENTS

The Clash of Issues

I know of no country in which there is so little independence of mind and real freedom of discussion as in America.

ALEXIS DE TOCQUEVILLE

We are the most perfect society now existing in the world. Here man is free as he ought to be. . . . Here the rewards of his industry follow with equal steps the progress of his labour; his labour is founded on the basis of nature, *self-interest*.

M. G. ST. JEAN DE CRÈVECŒUR

North America offers an unlimited field of liberty to the individual. It does not simply give him the opportunity; it forces him to employ all the faculties with which God has endowed him. The arena is open. . . . [A] cause of your greatness is the unlimited expansion of individual liberty.

BARON VON HÜBNER

The land of the free! This the land of the free! Why, if I say anything that displeases them, the free mob will lynch me, and that's my freedom. Free? Why, I have never been in any country where the individual has such an abject fear of his fellow countrymen. Because, as I say, they are free to lynch him the moment he shows he is not one of them.

D. H. LAWRENCE

What is common to all the other-directed people is that their contemporaries are the source of direction for the individual — either those known to him or those with whom he is indirectly acquainted, through friends and through the mass media. . . . This mode of keeping in touch with others permits a close behavioral conformity . . . through an exceptional sensitivity to the actions and wishes of others.

DAVID RIESMAN

What Riesman has called the central feature of the modern American character — other-direction — is, in fact, the dominant element in our national character through most of our history.

CARL N. DEGLER

One would be hard put to find today the "conformity" *Main Street* exacted of Carol Kennicott thirty years ago. With rising educational levels, more individuals are able to indulge a wider variety of interests. . . . No one in the United States defends conformity. Everyone is against it, and probably everyone always was.

DANIEL BELL

For more than a century we have lived with the contrasting images of the American character which Thomas Jefferson and Alexis de Tocqueville visualized. [One] of these images presented the American as . . . an independent individualist, the other a mass-dominated conformist; one an idealist, the other a materialist. . . . Is it possible to uncover common factors in these apparently contradictory images, and thus to make use of them both in our quest for a definition of the national character? For no matter whether either of these versions of the American is realistic as a type or image, there is no doubt that both of them reflect fundamental aspects of the American experience.

DAVID POTTER

I. TOCQUEVILLE AND THE AMERICAN PARADOX

Alexis de Tocqueville visited the United States in 1831 when he was twenty-six years old. The liberal French aristocrat came ostensibly to investigate America's prison system, but out of his nine-month stay emerged the most illuminating study of democracy ever written. Democracy in America *is less a book of observation of the United States than an abstract philosophical treatise on the nature of democracy, the example for which was furnished by America. Through the case of America, where the "equality of condition" had developed most fully, Tocqueville tried to sketch the character of democracy in general, to emphasize its strengths and its dangers. Since he believed that the democratic tide would inevitably sweep over Europe, Tocqueville wrote in the hope that his France, rather than trying to turn back this irresistible wave, would learn from the American experience what opportunities were offered and which hazards might be skirted.*

In the first selection from Democracy in America, *Tocqueville indicates how democracy breeds individualism and he shows the ways in which Americans may be regarded as individualists. In the second selection, however, he writes of the conformity which also characterized and threatened American life. He does this through his conception of "the tyranny of the majority" — the phrase by which many people characterize Tocqueville's entire argument. But the chief strength of his work lies in his ability to place both individualism and conformity into a more complex paradoxical model by which the American character might more completely be understood. In the final selection, then, we encounter his significant effort to explain why individualistic Americans feel the need to bow down slavishly not before the power of* The State *but before that of the opinion of the majority.*

Alexis de Tocqueville: DEMOCRACY IN AMERICA

DEMOCRACY AND INDIVIDUALISM

I HAVE shown how it is that in ages of equality every man seeks for his opinions within himself: I am now about to show how it is that, in the same ages, all his feelings are turned toward himself alone. *Individualism* is a novel expression to which a novel idea has given birth. Our fathers were only acquainted with egotism. Egotism is a passionate and exaggerated love of self, which leads a

From Alexis de Tocqueville, *Democracy in America* (New York: Henry G. Langley, 1845, 2 vols.), Vol. II, pp. 104–108.

man to connect everything with his own person, and to prefer himself to everything in the world. Individualism is a mature and calm feeling, which disposes each member of the community to sever himself from the mass of his fellow-creatures, and to draw apart with his family and his friends; so that, after he has thus formed a little circle of his own, he willingly leaves society at large to itself. Egotism originates in blind instinct: individualism proceeds from erroneous judgement more than from depraved feelings; it originates as much in the deficiencies of the mind as in the perversity of the heart.

Egotism blights the germ of all virtue: individualism, at first, only saps the virtues of public life; but, in the long run, it attacks and destroys all others, and is at length absorbed in downright egotism. Egotism is a vice as old as the world, which does not belong to one form of society more than to another: individualism is of democratic origin, and it threatens to spread in the same ratio as the equality of conditions.

Among aristocratic nations, as families remain for centuries in the same condition, often on the same spot, all generations become as it were contemporaneous. A man almost always knows his forefathers, and respects them: he thinks he already sees his remote descendants, and he loves them. He willingly imposes duties on himself toward the former and the latter; and he will frequently sacrifice his personal gratifications to those who went before and to those who will come after him.

Aristocratic institutions have, moreover, the effect of closely binding every man to several of his fellow-citizens. As the classes of an aristocratic people are strongly marked and permanent, each of them is regarded by its own members as a sort of lesser country, more tangible and more cherished than the country at large. As in aristocratic communities all the citizens occupy fixed positions, one above the other, the result is that each of them always sees a man above himself whose patronage is necessary to him, and below himself another man whose co-operation he may claim.

Men living in aristocratic ages are therefore almost always closely attached to something placed out of their own sphere, and they are often disposed to forget themselves. It is true that in those ages the notion of human fellowship is faint, and that men seldom think of sacrificing themselves for mankind; but they often sacrifice themselves for other men. In democratic ages, on the contrary, when the duties of each individual to the race are much more clear, devoted service to any one man becomes more rare; the bond of human affection is extended, but it is relaxed.

Among democratic nations new families are constantly springing up, others are constantly falling away, and all that remain change their condition; the woof of time is every instant broken, and the track of generations effaced. Those who went before are soon forgotten; of those who will come after no one has any idea: the interest of man is confined to those in close propinquity to himself.

As each class approximates to other classes, and intermingles with them, its members become indifferent and as strangers to one another. Aristocracy had made a chain of all the members of the community, from the peasant to the king: democracy breaks that chain, and severs every link of it.

As social conditions become more equal, the number of persons increases who, although they are neither rich enough nor powerful enough to exercise any great influence over their fellow-creatures, have nevertheless acquired or retained sufficient education and fortune to satisfy their own wants. They owe nothing to any man, they expect nothing from any man; they acquire the habit of always considering themselves as standing alone, and they are apt to imagine that their whole destiny is in their own hands.

Thus not only does democracy make every man forget his ancestors, but it hides his descendants, and separates his contemporaries, from him; it throws him back forever upon himself alone, and threatens in the end to confine him entirely within the solitude of his own heart.

* * *

The period when the construction of democratic society upon the ruins of an aristocracy has just been completed, is especially that at which this separation of men from one another, and the egotism resulting from it, most forcibly strike the observation. Democratic communities not only contain a large number of independent citizens, but they are constantly filled with men who, having entered but yesterday upon their independent condition, are intoxicated with their new power. They entertain a presumptuous confidence in their strength, and as they do not suppose that they can henceforward ever have occasion to claim the assistance of their fellow-creatures, they do not scruple to show that they care for nobody but themselves.

An aristocracy seldom yields without a protracted struggle, in the course of which implacable animosities are kindled between the different classes of society. These passions survive the victory, and traces of them may be observed in the midst of the democratic confusion which ensues.

Those members of the community who were at the top of the late gradations of rank cannot immediately forget their former greatness; they will long regard themselves as aliens in the midst of the newly composed society. They look upon all those whom this state of society has made their equals as oppressors, whose destiny can excite no sympathy; they have lost sight of their former equals, and feel no longer bound by a common interest to their fate: each of them, standing aloof, thinks that he is reduced to care for himself alone. Those, on the contrary, who were formerly at the foot of the social scale, and who have been brought up to the common level by a sudden revolution, cannot enjoy their newly acquired independence without secret uneasiness; and if they meet with some of their former superiors on the same footing as themselves, they stand aloof from them with an expression of triumph and of fear.

It is, then, commonly at the outset of democratic society that citizens are most disposed to live apart. Democracy leads men not to draw near to their fellow-creatures; but democratic revolutions lead them to shun each other, and perpetuate in a state of equality the animosities which the state of inequality engendered.

The great advantage of the Americans is that they have arrived at a state of democracy without having to endure a democratic revolution; and that they are born equal, instead of becoming so.

* * *

THE TYRANNY OF THE MAJORITY

IT IS IN the examination of the display of public opinion in the United States, that we clearly perceive how far the power of the majority surpasses all the powers with which we are acquainted in Europe. Intellectual principles exercise an influence which is so invisible and often so inappreciable, that they baffle the toils of oppression. At the present time the most absolute monarchs in Europe are unable to prevent certain notions, which are opposed to their authority, from circulating in secret throughout their dominions, and even in their courts. Such is not the case in America; so long as the majority is still undecided, discussion is carried on; but as soon as its decision is irrevocably pronounced, a submissive silence is observed; and the friends, as well as the opponents of the measure, unite in assenting to its propriety. The reason of this is perfectly clear: no monarch is so absolute as to combine all the powers of society in his own hands, and to conquer all opposition, with the energy of a majority, which is invested with the right of making and of executing the laws.

The authority of a king is purely physical, and it controls the actions of the subject without subduing his private will; but the majority possesses a power which is physical and moral at the same time; it acts upon the will as well as upon the actions of men, and it represses not only all contest, but all controversy.

I know no country in which there is so little true independence of mind and freedom of discussion as in America. In any constitutional state in Europe every sort of religious and political theory may be advocated and propagated abroad; for there is no country in Europe so subdued by any single authority, as not to contain citizens who are ready to protect the man who raises his voice in the cause of truth, from the consequences of his hardihood. If he is unfortunate enough to live under an absolute government, the people is upon his side; if he inhabits a free country, he may find a shelter behind the authority of the throne, if he require one. The aristocratic part of society supports him in some countries, and the democracy in others. But in a nation where democratic institutions exist, organized like those of the United States, there is but one sole authority, one single element of strength and of success, with nothing beyond it.

In America, the majority raises very formidable barriers to the liberty of opinion: within these barriers an author may write whatever he pleases, but he will repent it if he ever step beyond them. Not that he is exposed to the terrors of an auto-da-fé, but he is tormented by the slights and persecutions of daily obloquy. His political career is closed for ever, since he has offended the only authority which is able to promote his success. Every sort of compensation, even that of celebrity, is refused to him. Before he published his opinions, he imagined that he held them in common with many others; but no sooner has he declared them openly, than he is loudly censured by his overbearing opponents, while those who think, without having the courage to speak, like him, abandon him in silence. He yields at length, oppressed by the daily efforts he has been making, and he

From Alexis de Tocqueville, *Democracy in America* (New York: Henry P. Langley, 1845, 2 vols.), Vol. I, pp. 284–289.

subsides into silence as if he was tormented by remorse for having spoken the truth.

Fetters and headsmen were the coarse instruments which tyranny formerly employed; but the civilization of our age has refined the arts of despotism, which seemed however to have been sufficiently perfected before. The excesses of monarchical power had devised a variety of physical means of oppression; the democratic republics of the present day have rendered it as entirely an affair of the mind, as that will which it is intended to coerce. Under the absolute sway of an individual despot, the body was attacked in order to subdue the soul; and the soul escaped the blows which were directed against it, and rose superior to the attempt; but such is not the course adopted by tyranny in democratic republics; there the body is left free, and the soul is enslaved. The sovereign can no longer say, "You shall think as I do on pain of death;" but he says, "You are free to think differently from me, and to retain your life, your property, and all that you possess; but if such be your determination, you are henceforth an alien among your people. You may retain your civil rights, but they will be useless to you, for you will never be chosen by your fellow-citizens, if you solicit their suffrages; and they will affect to scorn you, if you solicit their esteem. You will remain among men, but you will be deprived of the rights of mankind. Your fellow-creatures will shun you like an impure being; and those who are most persuaded of your innocence will abandon you too, lest they should be shunned in their turn. Go in peace! I have given you your life, but it is an existence incomparably worse than death."

Absolute monarchies have thrown an odium upon despotism; let us beware lest democratic republics should restore oppression, and should render it less odious and less degrading in the eyes of the many, by making it still more onerous to the few.

Works have been published in the proudest nations of the Old World, expressly intended to censure the vices and deride the follies of the time; Labruyère inhabited the palace of Louis XIV when he composed his chapter upon the Great, and Molière criticised the courtiers in the very pieces which were acted before the court. But the ruling power in the United States is not to be made game of; the smallest reproach irritates its sensibility, and the slightest joke which has any foundation in truth renders it indignant; from the style of its language to the more solid virtues of its character, everything must be made the subject of encomium. No writer, whatever be his eminence, can escape from this tribute of adulation to his fellow-citizens. The majority lives in the perpetual exercise of self-applause; and there are certain truths which the Americans can only learn from strangers or from experience.

If great writers have not at present existed in America, the reason is very simply given in these facts; there can be no literary genius without freedom of opinion, and freedom of opinion does not exist in America. The inquisition has never been able to prevent a vast number of anti-religious books from circulating in Spain. The empire of the majority succeeds much better in the United States, since it actually removes the wish of publishing them. Unbelievers are to be met with in America, but, to say the truth, there is no public organ of infidelity. Attempts have been made by some governments to protect the morality of nations by prohibiting licentious books.

In the United States no one is punished for this sort of works, but no one is induced to write them; not because all the citizens are immaculate in their manners, but because the majority of the community is decent and orderly.

In these cases the advantages derived from the exercise of this power are unquestionable; and I am simply discussing the nature of the power itself. This irresistible authority is a constant fact, and its beneficent exercise is an accidental occurrence. . . .

The tendencies which I have just alluded to are as yet very slightly perceptible in political society; but they already begin to exercise an unfavourable influence upon the national character of the Americans. I am inclined to attribute the singular paucity of distinguished political characters to the ever-increasing activity of the despotism of the majority in the United States.

When the American revolution broke out, they arose in great numbers; for public opinion then served, not to tyrannize over, but to direct the exertions of individuals. Those celebrated men took a full part in the general agitation of mind common at that period, and they attained a high degree of personal fame, which was reflected back upon the nation, but which was by no means borrowed from it.

In absolute governments, the great nobles who are nearest to the throne flatter the passions of the sovereign, and voluntarily truckle to his caprices. But the mass of the nation does not degrade itself by servitude; it often submits from weakness, from habit, or from ignorance, and sometimes from loyalty. Some nations have been known to sacrifice their own desires to those of the sovereign with pleasure and with pride; thus exhibiting a sort of independence in the very act of submission. These peoples are

miserable, but they are not degraded. There is a great difference between doing what one does not approve, and feigning to approve what one does; the one is the necessary case of a weak person, the other befits the temper of a lackey.

In free countries, where every one is more or less called upon to give his opinion in the affairs of state; in democratic republics, where public life is incessantly commingled with domestic affairs, where the sovereign authority is accessible on every side, and where its attention can almost always be attracted by vociferation, more persons are to be met with who speculate upon its foibles, and live at the cost of its passions, than in absolute monarchies. Not because men are naturally worse in these states than elsewhere, but the temptation is stronger, and of easier access at the same time. The result is a far more extensive debasement of the characters of citizens.

Democratic republics extend the practice of currying favour with the many, and they introduce it into a great number of classes at once; this is one of the most serious reproaches that can be addressed to them. In democratic states organized on the principles of the American republics, this is more especially the case, where the authority of the majority is so absolute and so irresistible, that a man must give up his rights as a citizen, and almost abjure his quality as a human being, if he intends to stray from the track which it lays down.

In that immense crowd which throngs the avenues to power in the United States, I found very few men who displayed any of that manly candour, and that masculine independence of opinion, which frequently distinguished the Americans in former times, and which constitute the leading feature in distin-

guished characters wheresoever they may
be found. It seems, at first sight, as if all
the minds of the Americans were formed
upon one model, so accurately do they
correspond in their manner of judging.
A stranger does, indeed, sometimes meet
with Americans who dissent from these
rigorous formularies; with men who deplore the defects of the laws, the mutability and the ignorance of democracy;
who even go so far as to observe the evil
tendencies which impair the national
character, and to point out such remedies
as it might be possible to apply; but no

one is there to hear these things beside
yourself, and you, to whom these secret
reflections are confided, are a stranger
and a bird of passage. They are very
ready to communicate truths which are
useless to you, but they continue to hold
a different language in public.

If ever these lines are read in America,
I am well assured of two things: in the
first place, that all who peruse them will
raise their voices to condemn me; and in
the second place, that very many of them
will acquit me at the bottom of their
conscience.

❁   ❁   ❁

INTELLECTUAL AUTHORITY AMONG A
DEMOCRATIC PEOPLE

AT DIFFERENT periods dogmatical
belief is more or less abundant. It
arises in different ways, and it may
change its object or its form; but under
no circumstances will dogmatical belief
cease to exist, or, in other words, men will
never cease to entertain some implicit
opinions without trying them by actual
discussion. If every one undertook to
form his own opinions, and to seek for
truth by isolated paths struck out by himself alone, it is not to be supposed that
any considerable number of men would
ever unite in any common belief.

But obviously without such common
belief no society can prosper — say rather
no society does subsist; for without ideas
held in common, there is no common action, and without common action, there
may still be men, but there is no social
body. In order that society should exist,
and, *a fortiori,* that a society should prosper, it is required that all the minds of

the citizens should be rallied and held
together by certain predominant ideas;
and this cannot be the case, unless each
of them sometimes draws his opinions
from the common source, and consents
to accept certain matters of belief at the
hands of the community.

If I now consider man in his isolated
capacity, I find that dogmatical belief is
not less indispensable to him in order to
live alone, than it is to enable him to
co-operate with his fellow creatures. If
man were forced to demonstrate to himself all the truths of which he makes daily
use, his task would never end. He would
exhaust his strength in preparatory exercises, without advancing beyond them.
As, from the shortness of his life, he has
not the time, nor, from the limits of his
intelligence, the capacity, to accomplish
this, he is reduced to take upon trust a
number of facts and opinions which he
has not had either the time or the power

From Alexis de Tocqueville, *Democracy in America* (New York: Henry G. Langley, 1845, 2 vols.),
Vol. II, pp. 7–11, 272–279.

to verify himself, but which men of greater ability have sought out, or which the world adopts. On this groundwork he raises for himself the structure of his own thoughts; nor is he led to proceed in this manner by choice, so much as he is constrained by the inflexible law of his condition.

There is no philosopher of such great parts in the world, but that he believes a million of things on the faith of other people, and supposes a great many more truths than he demonstrates.

This is not only necessary but desirable. A man who should undertake to inquire into everything for himself, could devote to each thing but little time and attention. His task would keep his mind in perpetual unrest, which would prevent him from penetrating to the depth of any truth, or of grappling his mind indissolubly to any conviction. His intellect would be at once independent and powerless. He must therefore make his choice from among the various objects of human belief, and he must adopt many opinions without discussion, in order to search the better into that smaller number which he sets apart for investigation. It is true, that whoever receives an opinion on the word of another, does so far enslave his mind; but it is a salutary servitude which allows him to make a good use of freedom.

A principle of authority must then always occur, under all circumstances, in some part or other of the moral and intellectual world. Its place is variable, but a place it necessarily has. The independence of individual minds may be greater or it may be less: unbounded it cannot be. Thus the question is, not to know whether any intellectual authority exists in the ages of democracy, but simply where it resides and by what standard it is to be measured.

I have shown in the preceding chapter how the equality of conditions leads men to entertain a sort of instinctive incredulity of the supernatural, and a very lofty and often exaggerated opinion of the human understanding. The men who live at a period of social equality are not therefore easily led to place that intellectual authority to which they bow either beyond or above humanity. They commonly seek for the sources of truth in themselves, or in those who are like themselves. This would be enough to prove that at such periods no new religion could be established, and that all schemes for such a purpose would be not only impious but absurd and irrational. It may be foreseen that a democratic people will not easily give credence to divine missions; that they will turn modern prophets to a ready jest; and that they will seek to discover the chief arbiter of their belief within, and not beyond the limits of their kind.

When the ranks of society are unequal, and men unlike each other in condition, there are some individuals invested with all the power of superior intelligence, learning, and enlightenment, while the multitude is sunk in ignorance and prejudice. Men living at these aristocratic periods are therefore naturally induced to shape their opinions by the superior standard of a person or a class of persons, while they are averse to recognise the infallibility of the mass of the people.

The contrary takes place in ages of equality. The nearer the citizens are drawn to the common level of an equal and similar condition, the less prone does each man become to place implicit faith in a certain man or a certain class of men. But his readiness to believe the multitude increases, and opinion is more than ever mistress of the world. Not only is common opinion the only guide which private judgement retains among a democratic people, but among such a people it possesses a power infinitely beyond what it has elsewhere. At periods of equality men have no faith in one another, by reason of their common resemblance; but this very resemblance gives them almost unbounded confidence in the judgement of the public; for it would not seem probable, as they are all endowed with equal means of judging, but that the greater truth should go with the greater number.

When the inhabitant of a democratic country compares himself individually with all those about him, he feels with pride that he is the equal of any one of them; but when he comes to survey the totality of his fellows, and to place himself in contrast to so huge a body, he is instantly overwhelmed by the sense of his own insignificance and weakness.

The same equality which renders him independent of each of his fellow-citizens, taken severally, exposes him alone and unprotected to the influence of the greater number.

The public has therefore among a democratic people a singular power, of which aristocratic nations could never so much as conceive an idea; for it does not persuade to certain opinions, but it enforces them, and infuses them into the faculties by a sort of enormous pressure of the minds of all upon the reason of each.

In the United States the majority undertakes to supply a multitude of ready-made opinions for the use of individuals, who are thus relieved from the necessity of forming opinions of their own. Every body there adopts great numbers of theories on philosophy, morals, and politics, without inquiry, upon public trust; and if we look to it very narrowly, it will be perceived that religion herself holds her sway there, much less as a doctrine of revelation than as a commonly received opinion.

The fact that the political laws of the Americans are such that the majority rules the community with sovereign sway, materially increases the power which that majority naturally exercises over the mind. For nothing is more customary in man than to recognise superior wisdom in the person of his oppressor. This political omnipotence of the majority in the United States doubtless augments the influence which public opinion would obtain without it over the mind of each member of the community; but the foundations of that influence do not rest upon it. They must be sought for in the principle of equality itself, not in the more or less popular institutions which men living under that condition may give themselves. The intellectual dominion of the greater number would probably be less absolute among a democratic people governed by a king than in the sphere of a pure democracy, but it will always be extremely absolute; and by whatever political laws men are governed in the ages of equality, it may be foreseen that faith in public opinion will become a species of religion there, and the majority its ministering prophet.

Thus intellectual authority will be different, but it will not be diminished; and far from thinking that it will disappear, I augur that it may readily acquire too much preponderance, and confine the action of private judgement within narrower limits than are suited either to the greatness or the happiness of the human race. In the principle of equality I very clearly discern two tendencies; the one leading the mind of every man to untried thoughts, the other inclined to prohibit him from thinking at all. And I perceive how, under the dominion of certain laws, democracy would extinguish that liberty of the mind to which a democratic social condition is favorable; so that, after having broken all the bondage once imposed on it by ranks or by men, the human mind would be closely fettered to the general will of the greatest number.

If the absolute power of a majority were to be substituted by democratic nations, for all the different powers which checked or retarded overmuch the energy of individual minds, the evil would only have changed its symptoms. Men would not have found the means of independent life; they would simply have invented (no easy task) a new dress for servitude. There is — and I cannot repeat it too often — there is in this matter for profound reflection for those who look on freedom as a holy thing, and who hate not only the despot, but despotism. For myself, when I feel the hand of power lie heavy on my brow, I care but little to know who oppresses me; and I am not the more disposed to pass beneath the yoke, because it is held out to me by the arms of a million men.

*   *   *

When social conditions are equal, every man is apt to live apart, centered in himself and forgetful of the public. If the rulers of democratic nations were either to neglect to correct this fatal tendency, or to encourage it from a notion that it weans men from political passions and thus wards off revolutions, they might eventually produce the evil they seek to avoid, and a time might come when the inordinate passions of a few men, aided by the unintelligent selfishness or the pusillanimity of the greater number, would ultimately compel society to pass through strange vicissitudes. In democratic communities revolutions are seldom desired except by a minority; but a minority may sometimes effect them.

I do not assert that democratic nations are secure from revolutions; I merely say that the state of society in those nations does not lead to revolutions, but rather wards them off. A democratic people left to itself will not easily embark in great hazards; it is only led to revolutions unawares; it may sometimes undergo them, but it does not make them: and I will add that, when such a people has been allowed to acquire sufficient knowledge and experience, it will not suffer them to be made.

I am well aware that in this respect public institutions may themselves do much; they may encourage or repress the tendencies which originate in the state of society. I therefore do not maintain, I repeat, that a people is secure from revolutions simply because conditions are equal in the community; but I think that, whatever the institutions of such a people may be, great revolutions will always be far less violent and less frequent than is supposed; and I can easily discern a state of polity, which, when combined with the principle of equality, would render society more stationary than it has ever been in our western part of the world.

The observations I have here made on events may also be applied in part to opinions. Two things are surprising in the United States — the mutability of the greater part of human actions, and the singular stability of certain principles. Men are in constant motion; the mind of man appears almost unmoved. When once an opinion has spread over the country and struck root there, it would seem that no power on earth is strong enough to eradicate it. In the United States, general principles in religion, philosophy, morality, and even politics, do not vary, or at least are only modified by a hidden and often an imperceptible process: even the grossest prejudices are obliterated with incredible slowness, amid the continual friction of men and things.

I hear it said that it is in the nature and the habits of democracies to be constantly changing their opinions and feelings. This may be true of small democratic nations, like those of the ancient world, in which the whole community could be assembled in a public place and then excited at will by an orator. But I saw nothing of the kind among the great democratic people which dwells upon the opposite shores of the Atlantic ocean. What struck me in the United States was the difficulty of shaking the majority in an opinion once conceived, or of drawit off from a leader once adopted. Neither speaking nor writing can accomplish it; nothing but experience will avail, and even experience must be repeated.

This is surprising at first sight, but a more attentive investigation explains the fact. I do not think that it is as easy as is supposed to uproot the prejudices of a democratic people — to change its belief — to supersede principles once established, by new principles in religion, politics, and morals — in a word, to make great and frequent changes in men's minds. Not that the human mind is there at rest — it is in constant agitation; but it is engaged in infinitely varying the consequences of known principles, and in seeking for new consequences, rather than in seeking for new principles. Its motion is one of rapid circumvolution, rather than of straightforward impulse by rapid and direct effort; it extends its orbit by small continual and hasty movements, but it does not suddenly alter its position.

Men who are equal in rights, in education, in fortune, or, to comprise all in one word, in their social condition, have necessarily wants, habits and tastes which

are hardly dissimilar. As they look at objects under the same aspect, their minds naturally tend to analogous conclusions; and, though each of them may deviate from his contemporaries and form opinions of his own, they will involuntarily and unconsciously concur in a certain number of received opinions. The more attentively I consider the effects of equality upon the mind, the more am I persuaded that the intellectual anarchy which we witness about us is not, as many men suppose, the natural state of democratic nations. I think it is rather to be regarded as an accident peculiar to their youth, and that it only breaks out at that period of transition when men have already snapped the former ties which bound them together, but are still amazingly different in origin, education, and manners; so that, having retained opinions, propensities and tastes of great diversity, nothing any longer prevents men from avowing them openly. The leading opinions of men become similar in proportion as their conditions assimilate; such appears to me to be the general and permanent law — the rest is casual and transient.

I believe that it will rarely happen to any man among a democratic community, suddenly to frame a system of notions very remote from that which his contemporaries have adopted; and if some such innovator appeared, I apprehend that he would have great difficulty in finding listeners, still more in finding believers. When the conditions of men are almost equal, they do not easily allow themselves to be persuaded by each other. As they all live in close intercourse, as they have learned the same things together, and as they lead the same life, they are not naturally disposed to take one of themselves for a guide, and to follow him implicitly. Men seldom take the opinion of their equal, or of a man like themselves, upon trust.

Not only is confidence in the superior attainments of certain individuals weakened among democratic nations, as I have elsewhere remarked, but the general notion of the intellectual superiority which any man whatsoever may acquire in relation to the rest of the community is soon overshadowed. As men grow more like each other, the doctrine of the equality of the intellect gradually infuses itself into their opinions; and it becomes more difficult for any innovator to acquire or to exert much influence over the minds of a people. In such communities sudden intellectual revolutions will therefore be rare; for, if we read aright the history of the world, we shall find that great and rapid changes in human opinions have been produced far less by the force of reasoning than by the authority of a name.

Observe, too, that as the men who live in democratic societies are not connected with each other by any tie, each of them must be convinced individually; while in aristocratic society it is enough to convince a few — the rest follow. If Luther had lived in an age of equality, and had not had princes and potentates for his audience, he would perhaps have found it more difficult to change the aspect of Europe.

Not indeed that the men of democracies are naturally strongly persuaded of the certainty of their opinions, or are unwavering in belief; they frequently entertain doubts which no one, in their eyes, can remove. It sometimes happens at such times, that the human mind would willingly change its position; but as nothing urges or guides it forward, it oscillates to and fro without progressive motion.

Even when the reliance of a democratic people has been won, it is still no easy matter to gain their attention. It is extremely difficult to obtain a hearing from men living in democracies, unless it be to speak to them of themselves. They do not attend to the things said to them, because they are always fully engrossed with the things they are doing. For indeed few men are idle in democratic nations; life is passed in the midst of noise and excitement, and men are so engaged in acting that little time remains to them for thinking. I would especially remark that they are not only employed, but that they are passionately devoted to their employments. They are always in action, and each of their actions absorbs their faculties: the zeal which they display in business puts out the enthusiasm they might otherwise entertain for ideas.

I think that it is extremely difficult to excite the enthusiasm of a democratic people for any theory which has not a palpable, direct, and immediate connexion with the daily occupations of life: therefore they will not easily forsake their old opinions; for it is enthusiasm which flings the mind of men out of the beaten track, and effects the great revolutions of the intellect as well as the great revolutions of the political world.

Thus democratic nations have neither time nor taste to go in search of novel opinions. Even when those they possess become doubtful, they still retain them, because it would take too much time and inquiry to change them — they retain them, not as certain, but as established....

If the influence of individuals is weak and hardly perceptible among such a people, the power exercised by the mass upon the mind of each individual is extremely great — I have already shown for what reasons. I would now observe that it is wrong to suppose that this depends solely upon the form of government, and that the majority would lose its intellectual supremacy if it were to lose its political power.

In aristocracies men have often much greatness and strength of their own: when they find themselves at variance with the greater number of their fellow-countrymen, they withdraw to their own circle, where they support and console themselves. Such is not the case in a democratic country; there, public favour seems as necessary as the air we breathe, and to live at variance with the multitude is, as it were, not to live. The multitude requires no laws to coerce those who think not like itself: public disapprobation is enough; a sense of their loneliness and impotence overtakes them and drives them to despair.

Whenever social conditions are equal, public opinion presses with enormous weight upon the minds of each individual; it surrounds, directs, and oppresses him; and this arises from the very constitution of society, much more than from its political laws. As men grow more alike, each man feels himself weaker in regard to all the rest; as he discerns nothing by which he is considerably raised above them, or distinguished from them, he mistrusts himself as soon as they assail him. Not only does he mistrust his strength, but he even doubts of his right; and he is very near acknowledging that he is in the wrong, when the greater number of his countrymen assert that he is so. The majority do not need to constrain him — they convince him. In whatever way then the powers of a democratic community may be organized and balanced, it will always be extremely difficult to believe what the bulk of the people reject, or to profess what they condemn.

This circumstance is extraordinarily favourable to the stability of opinions.

When an opinion has taken root among a democratic people, and established itself in the minds of the bulk of the community, it afterward subsists by itself and is maintained without effort, because no one attacks it. Those who at first rejected it as false, ultimately receive it as the general impression; and those who still dispute it in their hearts, conceal their dissent; they are careful not to engage in a dangerous and useless conflict.

It is true, that when the majority of a democratic people change their opinions, they may suddenly and arbitrarily effect strange revolutions in men's minds; but their opinions do not change without much difficulty, and it is almost as difficult to show that they are changed.

Time, events, or the unaided individual action of the mind, will sometimes undermine or destroy an opinion, without any outward sign of the change. It has not been openly assailed, no conspiracy has been formed to make war on it, but its followers one by one noiselessly secede — day by day a few of them abandon it, until at last it is only professed by a minority. In this state it will still continue to prevail. As its enemies remain mute, or only interchange their thoughts by stealth, they are themselves unaware for a long period that a great revolution has actually been effected; and in this state of uncertainty they take no steps — they observe each other, and are silent. The majority have ceased to believe what they believed before; but they still affect to believe, and this empty phantom of public opinion is strong enough to chill innovators, and to keep them silent and at a respectful distance.

We live at a time which has witnessed the most rapid changes of opinion in the minds of men; nevertheless it may be that the leading opinions of society will ere long be more settled than they have been for several centuries in our history: that time is not yet come, but it may perhaps be approaching. As I examine more closely the natural wants and tendencies of democratic nations, I grow persuaded that if ever social equality is generally and permanently established in the world, great intellectual and political revolutions will become more difficult and less frequent than is supposed. Because the men of democracies appear always excited, uncertain, eager, changeable in their wills and in their positions, it is imagined that they are suddenly to abrogate their laws, to adopt new opinions, and to assume new manners. But if the principle of equality predisposes men to change, it also suggests to them certain interests and tastes which cannot be satisfied without a settled order of things; equality urges them on, but at the same time it holds them back; it spurs them, but fastens them to earth; — it kindles their desires, but limits their powers.

This, however, is not perceived at first; the passions which tend to sever the citizens of a democracy are obvious enough; but the hidden force which restrains and unites them is not discernable at a glance.

II. SOURCES OF INDIVIDUALISM

M. G. St. Jean de Crèvecœur: THE AMERICAN, THIS NEW MAN

At a time when Rousseau was celebrating the "noble savage," Michel-Guillaume de Crèvecœur's Letters from an American Farmer *struck an appropriate note. For here in the New World was being created a new man freed from the shackles and burdens of the European past and its institutions. Written during the 1770's by a Frenchman who took up farming in Orange County, New York, in 1765 (where he remained until the American Revolution), these letters enthusiastically portray free men working the earth, responsible only to God and to themselves. The source of their freedom to pursue enlightened self-interest lay in their escape from the bondage of European tradition into a new continent where one's own efforts could bring a man dignity.*

I WISH I could be acquainted with the feelings and thoughts which must agitate the heart and present themselves to the mind of an enlightened Englishman, when he first lands on this continent. He must greatly rejoice that he lived at a time to see this fair country discovered and settled; he must necessarily feel a share of national pride, when he views the chain of settlements which embellishes these extended shores. When he says to himself, this is the work of my countrymen, who, when convulsed by factions, afflicted by a variety of miseries and wants, restless and impatient, took refuge here. They brought along with them their national genius, to which they principally owe what liberty they enjoy, and what substance they possess. Here he sees the industry of his native country displayed in a new manner, and traces in their works the embryos of all the arts, sciences, and ingenuity which flourish in Europe. Here he beholds fair cities, substantial villages, extensive fields, an immense country filled with decent houses, good roads, orchards, meadows, and bridges, where an hundred years ago all was wild, woody, and uncultivated! What a train of pleasing ideas this fair spectacle must suggest; it is a prospect which must inspire a good citizen with the most heartfelt pleasure. The difficulty consists in the manner of viewing so extensive a scene. He is arrived on a new continent; a modern society offers itself to his contemplation, different from what he had hitherto seen. It is not composed, as in Europe, of great lords who possess everything, and of a herd of people who have nothing. Here are no aristocratical families, no courts, no kings, no bishops, no ecclesiastical dominion, no invisible power giving to a few a very visible one; no great manufacturers employing thousands, no great refinements of luxury. The rich and the poor are not so far removed from each other as they are in Europe. Some few towns excepted, we are all tillers of the earth, from Nova Scotia to West Florida. We are a people of cultivators, scattered over an immense

From M. G. St. Jean de Crèvecœur, *Letters from an American Farmer* (New York: Fox, Duffield, and Company, 1904), pp. 48–56.

territory, communicating with each other by means of good roads and navigable rivers, united by the silken bands of mild government, all respecting the laws, without dreading their power, because they are equitable. We are all animated with the spirit of an industry which is unfettered and unrestrained, because each person works for himself. If he travels through our rural districts he views not the hostile castle, and the haughty mansion, contrasted with the clay-built hut and miserable cabin, where cattle and men help to keep each other warm, and dwell in meanness, smoke, and indigence. A pleasing uniformity of decent competence appears throughout our habitations. The meanest of our log-houses is a dry and comfortable habitation. Lawyer or merchant are the fairest titles our towns afford; that of a farmer is the only appellation of the rural inhabitants of our country. It must take some time ere he can reconcile himself to our dictionary, which is but short in words of dignity, and names of honour. There, on a Sunday, he sees a congregation of respectable farmers and their wives, all clad in neat homespun, well mounted, or riding in their own humble waggons. There is not among them an esquire, saving the unlettered magistrate. There he sees a parson as simple as his flock, a farmer who does not riot on the labour of others. We have no princes, for whom we toil, starve, and bleed: we are the most perfect society now existing in the world. Here man is free as he ought to be; nor is this pleasing equality so transitory as many others are. Many ages will not see the shores of our great lakes replenished with inland nations, nor the unknown bounds of North America entirely peopled. Who can tell how far it extends? Who can tell the millions of men whom it will feed and contain? for no European

foot has as yet travelled half the extent of this mighty continent!

The next wish of this traveller will be to know whence came all these people? they are a mixture of English, Scotch, Irish, French, Dutch, Germans, and Swedes. From this promiscuous breed, that race now called Americans have arisen. The eastern provinces must indeed be excepted, as being the unmixed descendants of Englishmen. I have heard many wish that they had been more intermixed also: for my part, I am no wisher, and think it much better as it has happened. They exhibit a most conspicuous figure in this great and variegated picture; they too enter for a great share in the pleasing perspective displayed in these thirteen provinces. I know it is fashionable to reflect on them, but I respect them for what they have done; for the accuracy and wisdom with which they have settled their territory; for the decency of their manners; for their early love of letters; their ancient college, the first in this hemisphere; for their industry; which to me who am but a farmer, is the criterion of everything. There never was a people, situated as they are, who with so ungrateful a soil have done more in so short a time. Do you think that the monarchical ingredients which are more prevalent in other governments, have purged them from all foul stains? Their histories assert the contrary.

In this great American asylum, the poor of Europe have by some means met together, and in consequence of various causes; to what purpose should they ask one another what countrymen they are? Alas, two thirds of them had no country. Can a wretch who wanders about, who works and starves, whose life is a continual scene of sore affliction or pinching penury; can that man call England or any other kingdom his country? A country that had no bread for him, whose fields procured him no harvest, who met with nothing but the frowns of the rich, the severity of the laws, with jails and punishments; who owned not a single foot of the extensive surface of this planet? No! urged by a variety of motives, here they came. Every thing has tended to regenerate them; new laws, a new mode of living, a new social system; here they are become men: in Europe they were as so many useless plants, wanting vegetative mould, and refreshing showers; they withered, and were mowed down by want, hunger, and war; but now by the power of transplantation, like all other plants they have taken root and flourished! Formerly they were not numbered in any civil lists of their country, except in those of the poor; here they rank as citizens. By what invisible power has this surprising metamorphosis been performed? By that of the laws and that of their industry. The laws, the indulgent laws, protect them as they arrive, stamping on them the symbol of adoption; they receive ample rewards for their labours; these accumulated rewards procure them lands; those lands confer on them the title of freemen, and to that title every benefit is affixed which men can possibly require. This is the great operation daily performed by our laws. From whence proceed these laws? From our government. Whence the government? It is derived from the original genius and strong desire of the people ratified and confirmed by the crown. This is the great chain which links us all, this is the picture which every province exhibits, Nova Scotia excepted. There the crown has done all; either there were no people who had genius, or it was not much attended to: the consequence is, that the province is very thinly inhabited indeed; the power of the crown in conjunction with the musketos has prevented men from settling there. Yet some parts of it flourished once, and it contained a mild harmless set of people. But for the fault of a few leaders, the whole were banished. The greatest political error the crown ever committed in America, was to cut off men from a country which wanted nothing but men!

What attachment can a poor European emigrant have for a country where he had nothing? The knowledge of the language, the love of a few kindred as poor as himself, were the only cords that tied him: his country is now that which gives him land, bread, protection, and consequence: *Ubi panis ibi patria,* is the motto of all emigrants. What then is the American, this new man? He is either an European, or the descendant of an European, hence that strange mixture of blood, which you will find in no other country. I could point out to you a family whose grandfather was an Englishman, whose wife was Dutch, whose son married a French woman, and whose present four sons have now four wives of different nations. *He* is an American, who, leaving behind him all his ancient prejudices and manners, receives new ones from the new mode of life he has embraced, the new government he obeys, and the new rank he holds. He becomes an American by being received in the broad lap of our great *Alma Mater.* Here individuals of all nations are melted into a new race of men, whose labours and posterity will one day cause great changes in the world. Americans are the western pilgrims, who are carrying along with them that great mass of arts, sciences, vigour, and industry which began long since in the east; they will finish the great circle. The Americans were once scattered all over Europe; here they are incorporated into one of the finest systems of population which has ever appeared, and which will hereafter become distinct by the power of the different climates they inhabit. The American ought therefore to love this country much better than that wherein either he or his forefathers were born. Here the rewards of his industry follow with equal steps the progress of his labour; his labour is founded on the basis of nature, *self-interest;* can it want a stronger allurement? Wives and children, who before in vain demanded of him a morsel of bread, now, fat and frolicsome, gladly help their father to clear those fields whence exuberant crops are to arise to feed and to clothe them all; without any part being claimed, either by a despotic prince, a rich abbot, or a mighty lord. Here religion demands but little of him; a small voluntary salary to the minister, and gratitude to God; can he refuse these? The American is a new man, who acts upon new principles; he must therefore entertain new ideas, and form new opinions. From involuntary idleness, servile dependence, penury, and useless labour, he has passed to toils of a very different nature, rewarded by ample subsistence. — This is an American.

Thomas Jefferson: THE MORAL INDEPENDENCE OF THE CULTIVATOR OF THE EARTH

Thomas Jefferson wrote his Notes on the State of Virginia *in 1781. Query XIX, dealing with manufactures, serves as Jefferson's vehicle for connecting agriculture with moral independence and for associating city mobs with degeneracy. These assumptions have colored much subsequent American history and have furnished Americans with an attitude which, however questionable it might be, lives on still.*

WE NEVER had an interior trade of any importance. Our exterior commerce has suffered very much from the beginning of the present contest. During this time we have manufactured within our families the most necessary articles of cloathing. Those of cotton will bear some comparison with the same kinds of manufacture in Europe; but those of wool, flax and hemp are very coarse, unsightly, and unpleasant: and such is our attachment to agriculture, and such our preference for foreign manufactures, that be it wise or unwise, our people will certainly return as soon as they can, to the raising raw materials, and exchanging them for finer manufactures than they are able to execute themselves.

The political œconomists of Europe have established it as a principle that every state should endeavour to manufacture for itself: and this principle, like many others, we transfer to America, without calculating the difference of circumstance which should often produce a difference of result. In Europe the lands are either cultivated, or locked up against the cultivator. Manufacture must therefore be resorted to of necessity not of choice, to support the surplus of their people. But we have an immensity of land courting the industry of the hus-

From Thomas Jefferson, *Notes on the State of Virginia* (Richmond, 1853), Query XIX.

bandman. Is it best then that all our citizens should be employed in its improvement, or that one half should be called off from that to exercise manufactures and handicraft arts for the other? Those who labour in the earth are the chosen people of God, if ever he had a chosen people, whose breasts he has made his peculiar deposit for substantial and genuine virtue. It is the focus in which he keeps alive that sacred fire, which otherwise might escape from the face of the earth. Corruption of morals in the mass of cultivators is a phænomenon of which no age nor nation has furnished an example. It is the mark set on those, who not looking up to heaven, to their own soil and industry, as does the husbandman, for their subsistence, depend for it on the casualties and caprice of customers. Dependance begets subservience and venality, suffocates the germ of virtue, and prepares fit tools for the designs of ambition. This, the natural progress and consequence of the arts, has sometimes perhaps been retarded by accidental circumstances: but, generally speaking, the proportion which the aggregate of the other classes of citizens bears in any state to that of its husbandmen, is the proportion of its unsound to its healthy parts, and is a good-enough barometer whereby to measure its degree of corruption. While we have land to labour then, let us never wish to see our citizens occupied at a work-bench, or twirling a distaff. Carpenters, masons, smiths, are wanting in husbandry: but, for the general operations of manufacture, let our work-shops remain in Europe. It is better to carry provisions and materials to workmen there, than bring them to the provisions and materials, and with them their manners and principles. The loss by the transportation of commodities across the Atlantic will be made up in happiness and permanence of government. The mobs of great cities add just so much to the support of pure government, as sores do to the strength of the human body. It is the manners and spirit of a people which preserve a republic in vigour. A degeneracy in these is a canker which soon eats to the heart of its laws and constitution.

Harriet Martineau: CONFORMITY IN THE EAST AND INDIVIDUALISM IN THE WEST

When manufacturing and industry reshaped the life of the populous north-eastern seaboard in the first half of the nineteenth century it became fairly common to look to the relatively unsettled West for the seedbed and fruits of individualism. This was a logical consequence of the Jeffersonian position. The illustrious English reformer Harriet Martineau traveled around the United States for two years beginning in 1834. She had the perspicacity to note in American life elements both of individualism and conformity, but unlike Tocqueville who worked them both into a complex model of the American character (his study first appeared in 1835), Miss Martineau saw the two characteristics as being divided roughly along geographical lines. Although Miss Martineau's case is not exactly parallel, there has been a tendency

among many American historians to view the American character in
similarly schizoid terms, divided between its liberal super-ego and its
conservative id, with one gaining the ascendancy for a time and then
the other. These analysts have usually been labeled "progressive his-
torians," and there is much in the observations and conceptualizations
found in Miss Martineau's books to give support to these scholars.

IF ANY American were trusted by his countrymen to delineate what they call their national character, it would infallibly come out a perfect likeness of Washington. But there is a mistake here. There were influences prior to Washington, and there are circumstances which have survived him, that cause some images to lie deeper down in the hearts of Americans than Washington himself. His character is a grand and very prevalent idea among them: but there are others which take the precedence, from being more general still. Wealth and opinion were practically worshipped before Washington opened his eyes on the sun which was to light him to his deeds; and the worship of Opinion is, at this day, the established religion of the United States.

If the prevalent idea of society did not arise out of circumstances over which the mutations of outward events exercise but a small immediate influence, it is clear that, in this case, the idea should arise out of the characters of the benefactors who achieved the revolution, and must be consistent with the solemn words in which they conveyed their united Declaration. The principles of truth, and the rule of justice, according to which that Declaration was framed, and that revolutionary struggle undertaken and conducted, should, but for prior influences, have been the spirit inspiring the whole civilisation of the American people. There should then have been the utmost social as well as political freedom. The pursuit

of wealth might then have been subordinated at pleasure: fear of injury, alike from opinion and from violence, should have been banished; and as noble facilities afforded for the progression of the inward, as for the enjoyment of the outward, man. But this was not given. Instead of it there was ordained a mingling of old and new influences, from which a somewhat new kind of civilisation has arisen.

The old-world estimation of wealth has remained among them, though, I believe and trust, somewhat diminished in strength. Though every man works for it in America, and not quite every man does so in England, it seems to me that it is not so absolutely the foreground object in all views of life, the one subject of care, speculation, inquiry, and supposition, that it is in England. It is in America clearly subordinate to another idea, still an idol, but of a higher order than the former. The worship of Opinion certainly takes precedence of that of wealth.

In a country where the will of the majority decides all political affairs, there is a temptation to belong to the majority, except where strong interests, or probabilities of the speedy supremacy of the minority, countervail. The minority, in such a case, must be possessed of a strong will, to be a minority. A strong will is dreaded by the weaker, who have so little faith as to believe that such a will endangers the political equality which is the fundamental principle of their institu-

From Harriet Martineau, *Society in America* (London: Saunders and Otley, 1837, 3 vols.), Vol. III, pp. 6–9, 21–23.

tions. This dread occasions persecution, or at least opprobrium: opprobrium becomes a real danger; and, like all dangers, is much more feared than it deserves, the longer it lasts, and the more it is dwelt upon. Thus, from a want of faith in the infallible operation of the principles of truth and the rule of justice, these last become "hollow words" in the States of the new, as in the kingdoms of the old world; and the infant nation, which was expected to begin a fresh and higher social life, is acting out in its civilisation an idea but little more exalted than those which have operated among nations far less favoured than herself in regard to political freedom. . . .

The traveller should go into the west when he desires to see universal freedom of manners. The people of the west have a comfortable self-complacency, equally different from the arrogance of the south, and the timidity of the north. They seem to unite with this the hospitality which distinguishes the whole country: so that they are, on the whole, a very bewitching people. Their self-confidence probably arises from their being really remarkably energetic, and having testified this by the conquests over nature which their mere settlement in the west evinces. They are the freest people I saw in America: and accordingly one enjoys among them a delightful exemption from the sorrow and indignation which worldly caution always inspires; and from flattery. If the stranger finds himself flattered in the west, he may pretty safely conclude that the person he is talking with comes from New England. "We are apt to think," said a westerner to me, "that however great and good another person may be, we are just as great and good." Accordingly, intercourse goes on without any reference whatever to the merits of the respective parties. In the sunshine of complacency,

their free thoughts ripen into free deeds, and the world gains largely. There are, naturally, instances of extreme conceit, here and there: but I do not hesitate to avow that, prevalent as mock-modesty and moral cowardice are in the present condition of society, that degree of self-confidence which is commonly called conceit grows in favour with me perpetually. An over-estimate of self appears to me a far less hurtful and disagreeable mistake than the idolatry of opinion. It is a mistake which is sure to be rectified, sooner or later; and very often, it proves to be no mistake where small critics feel the most confident that they may safely ridicule it. The event decides this matter of self-estimate, beyond all question; and while the event remains undisclosed, it is easy and pleasant to give men credit for as much as they believe themselves to be capable of: — more easy and pleasant than to see men restricting their own powers by such calculation of consequences as implies an equal want of faith in others and in themselves. If John Milton were now here to avow his hope that he should produce that which "the world would not willingly let die," what a shout there would be of "the conceited fellow!" while, the declaration having been made venerable by the event, it is now cited as an instance of the noble self-confidence of genius.

The people of the west have a right to so much self-confidence as arises from an ascertainment of what they can actually achieve. They come from afar, with some qualities which have force enough to guide them into a new region. They subdue this region to their own purposes; and, if they do often forget that the world elsewhere is progressing; if they do suppose themselves as relatively great in present society as they were formerly in the wilderness, it should be remembered, on their behalf, that they have effectually asserted their manhood in the conquest of circumstances.

If we are not yet to see, except in individual instances, the exquisite union of fearlessness with modesty, of self-confidence with meekness; — if there must be either the love of being grand in one's own eyes, or the fear of being little in other people's, — the friends of the Americans would wish that their error should be that which is allied to too much, rather than too little freedom.

The Baron J. A. Graf von Hübner: INDIVIDUALISM AS A FUNCTION OF OPPORTUNITY

The Baron von Hübner did not idolize the common man. As a distinguished Austrian Ambassador to France and Italy between 1849 and 1868, and later as a conservative representative in the Austrian Reichsrat, he viewed the United States from the special perspective of the Old World aristocrat. Thus it should occasion no surprise that when he found that the individual had been liberated in the America of 1871, that opportunity had been granted him and even imposed upon him, the Baron did not find in this a cause for unqualified celebration. His critical judgments are thoughtful, however, and they deserve the serious attention of Americans.

IF WE, children of old Europe, we, who without shutting the door on the progress which is to modify our future, cling to the present, and to the logical, natural continuation of the past, to our old recollections, traditions and habits; if we do homage to your success, obtained under the shield of institutions which, on all essential points, are contrary to ours, this is a proof of our impartiality; and our praises are therefore the more flattering. For do not let us deceive ourselves — America is the born antagonist of Europe. I speak of the America of the United States, and of Europe such as she exists, such as she has been formed by the moulding of centuries; and not such as visionaries would like to fashion her, either after your image or after a model of their own invention. The first arrivals, the precursors of your actual greatness, those who sowed the seed, were discontented men. Intestine divisions and religious persecutions had torn them from their homes and thrown them on your shores. They brought with them and implanted in the soil of their new country the principle for which they had suffered and fought — the authority of the individual. He who possesses it is free in the fullest acceptation of the term. And, as in that sense, you are all free, each of you is the equal of the other. Your country, then, is the classic soil of liberty and equality, and it has become so from the fact of being peopled by the men whom Europe had expelled from its bosom. That is why you, in conformity with your recent origin, and we, by a totally different genesis which is lost in the night of

From Baron Graf von Hübner, *A Ramble Round the World, 1871* (London: Macmillan and Company, 1874, 2 vols.), Vol. 1, pp. 296–299, 306–307, 309–310.

time, are antagonistic. This antagonism is more apparent than real. Amongst yourselves you are neither so free nor so equal as we imagine in Europe; and the old society is not so hampered or divided into castes as you seem to think. But do not let us discuss this question. It would lead us too far; and as to our reciprocal convictions, they would go for nothing. I will content myself by saying that the more I travel and the older I grow, the more I am convinced that human beings and things everywhere resemble one another at bottom: and that the divergencies are principally on the surface. I see everywhere the same passions, the same aspirations, the same deceptions, and the same weaknesses. It is only the form which varies.

But you offer liberty and equality to everyone. It is to the magic charm of these two words, more than to your gold-fields, that you owe the influx of your emigrants, and the enormous and ever-growing increase of your population. Russia and Hungary have still miles of uncultivated lands. Algeria only needs and clamours for hands. But no one goes there. The English emigrate to Australia, because it is another England, and especially an England far more like you than the mother country. The great mass of emigrants, therefore, turn their steps to North America. Why? First, to find bread, an article which in our over-populated Europe it is no longer easy to procure; next, to obtain liberty and equality. I am not quite so sure whether you are able to offer them the latter, in proportion to their dreams of those two great blessings, which human nature, from its cradle, has so eagerly coveted. But you certainly offer them space. It is space which makes your fortune and which will make theirs; because you are endowed with all the qualities necessary to work

it, and the Celtic and German races possess the same and develop them through your teaching and example. For other countries do not lack space. The Pampas, for instance, and all those uncultivated regions of the republics of South America, are only waiting for men to develop their riches. But even without the obstacle of climate, the inhabitants are not up to the rugged struggle with nature, and although they too have inscribed on their banner the words "Liberty and Equality," the world is not thereby taken in. Soldiers of fortune, periodically defeated and replaced by rivals, equally hold in their hands this pretended liberty: and equality consists in submission to the will and caprices of these ephemeral masters. The emigrants, therefore, go to you. They seek, as I said before, for bread, individual liberty and social equality: and they find space, that is liberty to work, and equality of success, if they bring with them the necessary qualifications. . . .

North America offers an unlimited field of liberty to the individual. It does not only give him the opportunity: it forces him to employ all the faculties with which God has endowed him. The arena is open — as soon as he enters it he must fight, and fight to the death. In Europe it is just the contrary. Everyone finds himself hemmed in by the narrow sphere in which he is born. To get out of this groove, a man must be able to rise above his equals, to make extraordinary efforts, and to have both abilities and qualities above the average. What with you is the rule, with us is the exception. In Europe, if a man has fulfilled the duties of his state, which are always more or less limited by circumstances, and has obtained the ordinary reward for his labour (which reward is also limited by circumstances), he thinks he has amply answered to the requirements of his position. Why go out of the ordinary path? Why struggle for extraordinary objects when success is uncertain and the recompense small? Looking at the enormous competition, it is quite enough for him if he can gain a respectable livelihood. I don't say there are not some ambitious and restless spirits who make a noise in the world; but they are few compared to the masses of whom I am speaking. Let us give an example. I know a great country where manufactures would be capable of immense development. But if I were to exhort the principal manufacturers to augment their production, to introduce this or that machinery, so as to compete in the market with other countries, they would reply: "What would be the use? We have a sufficient market at home." They are content with small profits: small, I mean, in comparison with the immense gains they might make with a little more exertion. It is less trouble and less risk to go on in the old way. From this point of view, perhaps they are right; but the commerce of the nation remains below that of its neighbours.

Now in America, in every sphere of human activity, superhuman efforts are made. . . .

So much that is brilliant must have its dark shadow. Every mortal man is afflicted with the faults inseparable from his good qualities. And you are not exempt from this infirmity.

You have obtained, and are obtaining every day, enormous results; but it is at the cost of excessive labour, of a permanent tension of mind and an equally permanent drain of your physical strength. This excess of toil, of which I have already explained the reason, seems to me the source of serious evils. It must produce exhaustion, lassitude, and premature old age; it deprives those who give themselves up to it first, of time, and then of the power of enjoying the result of their labours. It makes gain — money, the principal object in life; excludes gaiety; entails a sadness which is the natural consequence of over-fatigue; and destroys the family tie and home joys. To observations such as these the same answer is invariably given. "Yes, it is true; but time will modify all this. We are at the working stage. We are making our fortunes — later on, will come the time of enjoyment and repose." I do not admit the truth of this reasoning. A sad and premature old age awaits men who have abused their strength. It is the same with individuals as with nations.

Another cause of your greatness is the unlimited expansion of individual liberty. But the liberty of the individual must necessarily be limited by the liberty of all represented by the State. From the balance of the two results their mutual guarantees. In the greater part of the countries of the Old World, the State claims too much and the individual obtains too little. With you, the fault is just the contrary. It is the conviction of most of your eminent men that you grant too much to the individual and too little to the State. The greater portion of the scandals and abuses which we see in your country arise from that source. The control of the organs of public opinion is insufficient. What is wanting, is the control of an admitted authority recognized by all the world.

Frederick Jackson Turner: THE FRONTIER AND INDIVIDUALISM

The American as individualist received scholarly sanction as the protagonist in Frederick Jackson Turner's famous frontier hypothesis, first enunciated in 1893 in the essay "The Significance of the Frontier in American History." Most people sensed that the individualistic American existed, but the frontier thesis made it easier to explain how he came into existence and why he was a peculiarly American product. Although the Turner thesis has come under considerable attack from historians in recent years, it is probably safe to say that to the extent that a people has any conscious awareness of their historical character, Americans to this day are in a rough sort of way still Turnerians and they conceive of their past in the terms given by Turner. His influence among practicing historians has not altogether vanished.

THE MOST important effect of the frontier has been in the promotion of democracy here and in Europe. As has been indicated, the frontier is productive of individualism. Complex society is precipitated by the wilderness into a kind of primitive organization based on the family. The tendency is anti-social. It produces antipathy to control, and particularly to any direct control. The tax-gatherer is viewed as a representative of oppression. Prof. Osgood, in an able article, has pointed out that the frontier conditions prevalent in the colonies are important factors in the explanation of the American Revolution, where individual liberty was sometimes confused with absence of all effective government. The same conditions aid in explaining the difficulty of instituting a strong government in the period of the confederacy. The frontier individualism has from the beginning promoted democracy.

The frontier States that came into the Union in the first quarter of a century of its existence came in with democratic suffrage provisions, and had reactive effects of the highest importance upon the older States whose people were being attracted there. An extension of the franchise became essential. It was *western* New York that forced an extension of suffrage in the constitutional convention of that State in 1821; and it was *western* Virginia that compelled the tide-water region to put a more liberal suffrage provision in the constitution framed in 1830, and to give to the frontier region a more nearly proportionate representation with the tide-water aristocracy. The rise of democracy as an effective force in the nation came in with western preponderance under Jackson and William Henry Harrison, and it meant the triumph of the frontier — with all of its good and with all of its evil elements. An interesting illustration of the tone of frontier democracy in 1830 comes from the same debates in the Virginia convention already referred to. A representative from western Virginia declared:

But, sir, it is not the increase of population in the West which this gentleman ought

From Frederick Jackson Turner, "Significance of the Frontier in American History," *Annual Report of the American Historical Association, 1893* (Washington, D. C.: Government Printing Office, 1894), pp. 221–223, 226–227.

to fear. It is the energy which the mountain breeze and western habits impart to those emigrants. They are regenerated, politically I mean, sir. They soon become *working politicians;* and the difference, sir, between a *talking* and a *working* politician is immense. The Old Dominion has long been celebrated for producing great orators; the ablest metaphysicians in policy; men that can split hairs in all abstruse questions of political economy. But at home, or when they return from Congress, they have negroes to fan them asleep. But a Pennsylvania, a New York, an Ohio, or a western Virginia statesman, though far inferior in logic, metaphysics, and rhetoric to an old Virginia statesman, has this advantage, that when he returns home he takes off his coat and takes hold of the plow. This gives him bone and muscle, sir, and preserves his republican principles pure and uncontaminated.

So long as free land exists, the opportunity for a competency exists, and economic power secures political power. But the democracy born of free land, strong in selfishness and individualism, intolerant of administrative experience and education, and pressing individual liberty beyond its proper bounds, has its dangers as well as its benefits. Individualism in America has allowed a laxity in regard to governmental affairs which has rendered possible the spoils system and all the manifest evils that follow from the lack of a highly developed civic spirit. In this connection may be noted also the influence of frontier conditions in permitting lax business honor, inflated paper currency and wild-cat banking. The colonial and revolutionary frontier was the region whence emanated many of the worst forms of an evil currency. The West in the War of 1812 repeated the phenomenon on the frontier of that day, while the speculation and wild-cat banking of the period of the crisis of 1837 occurred on the new frontier belt of the next tier of States. Thus each one of the periods of lax financial integrity coincides with periods when a new set of frontier communities had arisen, and coincides in area with these successive frontiers, for the most part. The recent Populist agitation is a case in point. Many a State that now declines any connection with the tenets of the Populists, itself adhered to such ideas in an earlier stage of the development of the State. A primitive society can hardly be expected to show the intelligent appreciation of the complexity of business interests in a developed society. The continual recurrence of these areas of paper-money agitation is another evidence that the frontier can be isolated and studied as a factor in American history of the highest importance. . . .

From the conditions of frontier life came intellectual traits of profound importance. The works of travelers along each frontier from colonial days onward describe certain common traits, and these traits have, while softening down, still persisted as survivals in the place of their origin, even when a higher social organization succeeded. The result is that to the frontier the American intellect owes its striking characteristics. That coarseness and strength combined with acuteness and inquisitiveness; that practical, inventive turn of mind, quick to find expedients; that masterful grasp of material things, lacking in the artistic but powerful to effect great ends; that restless, nervous energy; that dominant individualism, working for good and for evil, and withal that buoyancy and exuberance which comes with freedom — these are traits of the frontier, or traits called out elsewhere because of the existence of the frontier. Since the days when the fleet of Columbus sailed into the waters of the New World, America has been another name for opportunity, and the people of the United States have taken their tone from the incessant expansion which has not only been open but has even been forced upon them. He would be a rash prophet who should assert that the expansive character of American life has now entirely ceased. Movement has been its dominant fact, and, unless this training has no effect upon a people, the American energy will continually demand a wider field for its exercise. But never again will such gifts of free land offer themselves. For a moment, at the frontier, the bonds of custom are broken and unrestraint is triumphant. There is not *tabula rasa*. The stubborn American environment is there with its imperious summons to accept its conditions; the inherited ways of doing things are also there; and yet, in spite of environment, and in spite of custom, each frontier did indeed furnish a new field of opportunity, a gate of escape from the bondage of the past; and freshness, and confidence, and scorn of older society, impatience of its restraints and its ideas, and indifference to its lessons, have accompanied the frontier. What the Mediterranean Sea was to the Greeks, breaking the bond of custom, offering new experiences, calling out new institutions and activities, that, and more, the ever retreating frontier has been to the United States directly, and to the nations of Europe more remotely. And now, four centuries from the discovery of America, at the end of a hundred years of life under the Constitution, the frontier has gone, and with its going has closed the first period of American history.

III. SOURCES OF CONFORMITY

Edward Dicey: MASS EDUCATION AS THE SOURCE
OF AMERICAN UNIFORMITY

Whatever the social background of the European observers, the one American institution which came to be universally admired was public education and the idea of free compulsory schooling for all children, regardless of social background. Edward Dicey liked the United States and was, in fact, one of the few English newspapermen covering the Civil War to support the Union cause and the Northern way of life. His view, therefore, of mass education as a leading contributor to the regrettable intellectual conformity in American life commands our attention if only because of the author's reputation as a sympathetic and objective observer. This selection evolved from his experience on newspaper assignment in 1862. Dicey was for twenty years an editor of the London Observer.

IN A MORAL as opposed to a material point of view, the most striking feature about American society is its uniformity. Everybody, as a rule, holds the same opinions about everything, and expresses his views, more or less, in the same language. These views are often correct, almost invariably intelligent and creditable to the holders. But still, even at the risk of hearing paradoxes defended, you cannot help wishing, at times, for a little more of originality. I believe that this monotony in the tone of American talk and opinion arises from the universal diffusion of education. Everybody is educated up to a certain point, and very few are educated above it. They have all learned the same lessons under the same teachers, and, in consequence, share the same sentiments to a degree which it is difficult for an Englishman to appreciate beforehand. This monotony is infinitely more striking in the men than in the women. Ninety-nine American lads in a hundred go through exactly the same system of training. Up to eighteen or nineteen, they are carefully, if not very deeply, grounded in all the branches of a good ordinary English education. Then they go into business, and from that time their intellectual self-culture ceases. Unless they happen to travel, they have very little time for reading anything except the newspapers. The women pursue their education even after marriage, and are in consequence better read and more intellectual in their tastes than English ladies. In the long run, however, the national tone of mind is always derived from the male sex, and therefore the prevalent tone of America is not that of a highly educated society. I do not mean to say, for one moment, that there are not hundreds and thousands of men of really first-class education in the Northern States. On the contrary, some of the most thoroughly educated men it has been my lot to meet

From Edward Dicey, *Six Months in the Federal States* (London: Macmillan and Company, 1863, 2 vols.), Vol. I, pp. 305–310.

with have been Americans. I am speaking of the mass, not of individuals. This opinion of mine, if it is correct, explains a fact which otherwise would seem discouraging: I mean the small share taken by educated men — in our sense of the word — in American politics. The truth is that if America were governed to any great extent by politicians of classical education, the country would not be fairly represented by its rulers. It is not the case that the fact of a gentleman having received a refined culture is any disqualification to him in the eyes of the constituencies. On the other hand, it is a very small recommendation. I do not deny that this is, in itself, an evil; but the true nature of the evil is not that men of education are disqualified from entering a political career in America, but that they form so small a class that they possess no political influence. Just in the same way, there is no doubt that, relatively to the period, there were more highly educated men in the Union half a century ago than there are now. The early settlers in any new country bring with them a higher degree of individual culture than they can impart to their children. In the same ratio, however, that the education of the individual decreases, the average education of the mass increases, and, on the whole, the general tone of the nation gains in consequence. My friend, Mr. Holmes, once said to me: "We should find it very hard to match five thousand American gentlemen with five thousand English; but we could match five million ordinary Americans against the same number of your countrymen, without fear of the result." This explanation I believe to be the correct one with regard to the intellectual development of America.

The truth is the great mistake that we English make in judging of America is the assumption that the New World ought to be the reproduction of the Old Country. We expect our social system, our hierarchy of castes and rank, our forms of thought and feeling, to be repeated amongst a people growing up under conditions totally different from that in which we have been trained for hundreds of generations. Every departure from our own standard we consider to indicate moral degeneracy, while in reality it is only a symptom of development. No one who has lived in America can avoid coming to the conclusion that the Anglo-Saxon frame is gradually modifying itself to a form suited to the new conditions of climate and temperature under which it is called on to exist. What is true in the physical is true also in the moral world. By degrees the imported civilization and culture of the Old World are developing themselves into new forms and aspects. What will be the ultimate social system of America it is impossible to say. Never yet in history has a nation grown up under circumstances where all men have started equal, and where want and poverty have been practically unknown. That the product of these conditions will be a remarkable one, we are beginning to see already. I recollect a common Irishwoman I once traveled alongside of in the States, saying to me, when talking about her experience of her new home, "This is a blessed country, sir; I think God made it for the poor." And I have often fancied that this saying might be the clue to the future history of America.

I have been asked frequently, whether I should like to live in America — and to this question my answer has always been that that depends entirely upon circumstances. Men of highly educated tastes, used to the social pleasures of the Old World, will not find their wants gratified as easily and as fully in a new state of society as in an old. In fact, in plain English, if your tastes and your habits are those of men whose income is counted by hundreds, you had better stop where you are. But the man who has his living to earn is better off, in almost every respect, in America than he is in England. The very circumstances that render the United States unattractive as a residence for the man of wealth and refinement are a positive boon to those who possess neither of the attributes; and I am afraid that in this world the latter class is larger and more important than the former.

James Bryce: THE FATALISM OF THE MULTITUDE

If Tocqueville's Democracy in America *may be called the most brilliant treatise concerning this country written by a foreigner, then James Bryce's* The American Commonwealth *(1888) ranks as the most complete, most reliable, best-informed work in this genre. Where Tocqueville ingeniously speculated, Bryce meticulously observed and brought to bear a sympathetic understanding based upon extensive experience in this country. Bryce, who in 1907 became British Ambassador to the United States, denied Tocqueville had prophesied correctly when he issued his warnings about the tyranny of the majority; but Bryce also contended that closely related dangers were very real. He deplored the uniformity and monotony in American life and in explanation substituted for Tocqueville's "tyranny of the majority" a phrase with a similar rhythm and ring: "the fatalism of the multitude." Bryce's model of the American character is more complex and more indefinite than the following selection suggests, but he leans very heavily throughout his work on the ideas which the reader is about to encounter.*

ONE FEATURE of thought and sentiment in the United States needs special examination because it has been by most observers either ignored or confounded with a phenomenon which is at bottom quite different. This is a fatalistic attitude of mind, which, since it disposes men to acquiesce in the rule of numbers, has been, when perceived, attributed to or identified with what is commonly called the Tyranny of the Majority. The tendency to fatalism is never far from mankind. It is one of the first solutions of the riddle of the earth propounded by metaphysics. It is one of the last propounded by science. It has at all times formed the background to religions. No race is naturally less disposed to a fatalistic view of things than is the Anglo-American, with its restless self-reliant energy.

> Nil actum reputans dum quid restaret agendum,

its slender taste for introspection or meditation. Nevertheless, even in this people the conditions of life and politics have

From James Bryce, *The American Commonwealth* (New York: The Macmillan Company, 1893, 2 vols.), Vol. 2, pp. 344–353.

bred a sentiment or tendency which seems best described by the name of fatalism.

In small and rude communities, every free man, or at least every head of a household, feels his own significance and realizes his own independence. He relies on himself, he is little interfered with by neighbours or rulers. His will and his action count for something in the conduct of the affairs of the community he belongs to, yet common affairs are few compared to those in which he must depend on his own exertions. The most striking pictures of individualism that literature has preserved for us are those of the Homeric heroes, and of the even more terrible and self-reliant warriors of the Scandinavian sagas, men like Ragnar Lodbrog and Egil, son of Skallagrim, who did not regard even the gods, but trusted to their own might and main. In more developed states of society organized on an oligarchic basis, such as were the feudal kingdoms of the Middle Ages, or in socially aristocratic countries such as most parts of Europe have remained down to our own time, the bulk of the people are no doubt in a dependent condition, but each person derives a certain sense of personal consequence from the strength of his group and of the person or family at the head of it. Moreover, the upper class, being the class which thinks and writes, as well as leads in action, impresses its own type upon the character of the whole nation, and that type is still individualistic, with a strong consciousness of personal free will, and a tendency for each man, if not to think for himself, at least to value and to rely on his own opinion.

Let us suppose, however, that the aristocratic structure of society has been dissolved, that the old groups have disappeared, that men have come to feel themselves members rather of the nation than of classes, or families, or communities within the nation, that a levelling process has destroyed the ascendency of birth and rank, that large landed estates no longer exist, that many persons in what was previously the humbler class have acquired possession of property, that knowledge is easily accessible and the power of using it no longer confined to the few. Under such conditions of social equality the habit of intellectual command and individual self-confidence will have vanished from the leading class, which creates the type of national character, and will exist nowhere in the nation.

Let us suppose, further, that political equality has gone hand in hand with the levelling down of social eminence. Every citizen enjoys the same right of electing the representatives and officials, the same right of himself becoming a representative or an official. Every one is equally concerned in the conduct of public affairs, and since no man's opinion, however great his superiority in wealth, knowledge, or personal capacity, is legally entitled to any more weight than another's, no man is entitled to set special value on his own opinion, or to expect others to defer to it; for pretensions to authority will be promptly resented. All disputes are referred to the determination of the majority, there being no legal distinction between the naturally strong and naturally weak, between the rich and the poor, between the wise and the foolish. In such a state of things the strong man's self-confidence and sense of individual force will inevitably have been lowered, because he will feel that he is only one of many, that his vote or voice counts for no more than that of his neighbour, that he can prevail, if at all, only by keeping himself on a level with his neighbour and recognizing the latter's personality as being every whit equal to his own.

Suppose, further, that all this takes place in an enormously large and populous country, where the governing voters are counted by so many millions that each individual feels himself a mere drop in the ocean, the influence which he can exert privately, whether by his personal gifts or by his wealth, being confined to the small circle of his town or neighbourhood. On all sides there stretches round him an illimitable horizon; and beneath the blue vault which meets that horizon there is everywhere the same busy multitude with its clamour of mingled voices which he hears close by. In this multitude his own being seems lost. He has the sense of insignificance which overwhelms us when at night we survey the host of heaven, and know that from even the nearest fixed star this planet of ours is invisible.

In such a country, where complete political equality is strengthened and perfected by complete social equality, where the will of the majority is absolute, unquestioned, always invoked to decide every question, and where the numbers which decide are so vast that one comes to regard them as one regards the largely working forces of nature, we may expect to find certain feelings and beliefs dominant in the minds of men.

One of these is that the majority must prevail. All free government rests on this belief, for there is no other way of working free government. To obey the majority is, therefore, both a necessity and a duty, a duty because the alternative would be ruin and the breaking-up of laws.

Out of this dogma there grows up another which is less distinctly admitted, and indeed held rather implicitly than

consciously, that the majority is right. And out of both of these there grows again the feeling, still less consciously held, but not less truly operative, that it is vain to oppose or censure the majority.

It may seem that there is a long step from the first of these propositions to the second and third; and that, in fact, the very existence of a minority striving with a majority implies that there must be many who hold the majority to be wrong, and are prepared to resist it. Men do not at once abandon their views because they have been outvoted; they reiterate their views, they reorganize their party, they hope to prevail, and often do prevail in a subsequent trial of strength.

All this is doubtless involved in the very methods of popular government. But it is, nevertheless, true that the belief in the right of the majority lies very near to the belief that the majority must be right. As self-government is based on the notion that each man is more likely to be right than to be wrong, and that one man's opinion must be treated as equally good with another's, there is a presumption that when twenty thousand vote one way, and twenty-one thousand another, the view of the greater number is the better view. The habit of deference to a decision actually given strengthens this presumption, and weaves it into the texture of every mind. A conscientious citizen feels that he ought to obey the determination of the majority, and naturally prefers to think that which he obeys to be right. A citizen languidly interested in the question at issue finds it easier to comply with and adopt the view of the majority than to hold out against it. A small number of men with strong convictions or warm party feeling will, for a time, resist. But even they feel differently towards their cause after it has been defeated from what they did while it had still a prospect of success. They know that in the same proportion in which their supporters are dismayed, the majority is emboldened and confirmed in its views. It will be harder to fight a second battle than it was to fight the first, for there is (so to speak) a steeper slope of popular disapproval to be climbed. Thus, just as at the opening of a campaign, the event of the first collisions between the hostile armies has great significance, because the victory of one is taken as an omen and a presage by both, so in the struggles of parties success at an incidental election works powerfully to strengthen those who succeed, and depress those who fail, for it inspires self-confidence or self-distrust, and it turns the minds of waverers. The very obscurity of the causes which move opinion adds significance to the result. So in the United States, when the elections in any State precede by a few weeks a presidential contest, their effect has sometimes been so great as virtually to determine that contest by filling one side with hope and the other with despondency. Those who prefer to swim with the stream are numerous everywhere, and their votes have as much weight as the votes of the keenest partisans. A man of convictions may insist that the arguments on both sides are after the polling just what they were before. But the average man will repeat his arguments with less faith, less zeal, more of a secret fear that he may be wrong, than he did while the majority was still doubtful; and after every reassertion by the majority of its judgment, his knees grow feebler, till at last they refuse to carry him into the combat.

The larger the scale on which the majority works, the more potent are these tendencies. When the scene of action is a small commonwealth, the individual voters are many of them personally known to one another, and the motives which determine their votes are understood and discounted. When it is a moderately-sized country, the towns or districts which compose it are not too numerous for reckoning to overtake and imagination to picture them, and in many cases their action can be explained by well-known causes which may be represented as transitory. But when the theatre stretches itself to a continent, when the number of voters is counted by many millions, the wings of imagination droop, and the huge voting mass ceases to be thought of as merely so many individual human beings no wiser or better than one's own neighbours. The phenomenon seems to pass into the category of the phenomena of nature, governed by far-reaching and inexorable laws whose character science has only imperfectly ascertained, and which she can use only by obeying. It inspires a sort of awe, a sense of individual impotence, like that which man feels when he contemplates the majestic and eternal forces of the inanimate world. Such a feeling is even stronger when it operates, not on a cohesive minority which had lately hoped, or may yet hope, to become a majority, but on a single man or a small group of persons cherishing some opinion which the mass disapproves. Thus out of the mingled feelings that the multitude will prevail, and that the multitude, because it will prevail, must be right, there grows a self-distrust, a despondency, a disposition to fall into line, to acquiesce in the dominant opinion, to submit thought as well as action to the encompassing power of numbers. Now and then a resolute man will, like Athanasius, stand alone against the world. But such a man must have, like Athanasius, some special spring of inward strength; and the difficulty of winning over others against the overwhelming weight of the multitude will, even in such a man, dull the edge of enterprise. An individual seeking to make his view prevail, looks forth on his hostile fellow-countrymen as a solitary swimmer, raised high on a billow miles from land, looks over the countless waves that divide him from the shore, and quails to think how small the chance that his strength can bear him thither.

This tendency to acquiescence and submission, this sense of the insignificance of individual effort, this belief that the affairs of men are swayed by large forces whose movement may be studied but cannot be turned, I have ventured to call the Fatalism of the Multitude. It is often confounded with the tyranny of the majority, but is at bottom different, though, of course, its existence makes abuses of power by the majority easier, because less apt to be resented. But the fatalistic attitude I have been seeking to describe does not imply any exercise of power by the majority at all. It may rather seem to soften and make less odious such an exercise of power, may even dispense with that exercise, because it disposes a minority to submit without the need of a command, to spontaneously renounce its own view and fall in with the view which the majority has expressed. In the fatalism of the multitude there is neither legal nor moral compulsion; there is merely a loss of resisting power, a diminished sense of personal responsibility, and of the duty to battle for one's own opinions, such as has been bred in some peoples by the belief in an overmastering fate. It is true that the force to which the citizen of the vast democracy submits is a moral force, not that of an unapproachable Allah, nor of the unchangeable laws of matter. But it is a moral force acting on so vast a scale, and from causes often so obscure, that its effect on the mind of the individual may

well be compared with that which religious or scientific fatalism engenders.

No one will suppose that the above sketch is intended to apply literally to the United States, where in some matters legal restrictions check a majority, where local self-government gives the humblest citizen a sphere for public action, where individualism is still in many forms and directions so vigorous. An American explorer, an American settler in new lands, an American man of business pushing a great enterprise, is a being as bold and resourceful as the world has ever seen. All I seek to convey is that there are in the United States signs of such a fatalistic temper, signs which one must expect to find wherever a vast population governs itself under a system of complete social and political equality, and which may grow more frequent as time goes on.

There exist in the American Republic several conditions which specially tend to create such a temper.

One of these is the unbounded freedom of discussion. Every view, every line of policy, has its fair chance before the people. No one can say that audience has been denied him, and comfort himself with the hope that, when he is heard, the world will come round to him. Under a repressive government, the sense of grievance and injustice feeds the flame of resistance in a persecuted minority. But in a country like this, where the freedom of the press, the right of public meeting, and the right of association and agitation have been legally extended and are daily exerted, more widely than anywhere else in the world, there is nothing to awaken that sense. He whom the multitude condemns or ignores has no further court of appeal to look to. Rome has spoken. His cause has been heard and judgment has gone against him.

Another is the intense faith which the

Americans have in the soundness of their institutions, and in the future of their country. Foreign critics have said that they think themselves the special objects of the care of Divine Providence. If this be so, it is matter neither for surprise nor for sarcasm. They are a religious people. They are trying, and that on the largest scale, the most remarkable experiment in government the world has yet witnessed. They have more than once been surrounded by perils which affrighted the stoutest hearts, and they have escaped from these perils into peace and prosperity. There is among pious persons a deep conviction — one may often hear it expressed on platforms and from pulpits with evident sincerity — that God has specially chosen the nation to work out a higher type of civilization than any other State has yet attained, and that this great work will surely be brought to a happy issue by the protecting hand that has so long guided it. And, even when the feeling does not take a theological expression, the belief in what is called the "Mission of the Republic" for all humanity is scarcely less ardent. But the foundation of the Republic is confidence in the multitude, in its honesty and good sense, in the certainty of its arriving at right conclusions. Pessimism is the luxury of a handful; optimism is the private delight, as well as public profession, of nine hundred and ninety-nine out of every thousand, for nowhere does the individual associate himself more constantly and directly with the greatness of his country.

Now, such a faith in the people, and in the forces that sway them, disposes a man to acquiescence and submission. He cannot long hold that he is right and the multitude wrong. He cannot suppose that the country will ultimately suffer because it refuses to adopt what he urges upon it. As he comes of an energetic stock, he will use all proper means to state his views, and give them every chance of prevailing. But he submits more readily than an Englishman would do, ay, even to what an Englishman would think an injury to his private rights. When his legal right has been infringed, an American will confidently proceed to enforce at law his claim to redress, knowing that even against the government a just cause will prevail. But if he fails at law, the sense of his individual insignificance will still his voice. It may seem a trivial illustration to observe that when a railway train is late, or a waggon drawn up opposite a warehouse door stops the horse-car for five minutes, the passengers take the delay far more coolly and uncomplainingly than Englishmen would do. But the feeling is the same as that which makes good citizens bear with the tyranny of Bosses. It is all in the course of nature. Others submit; why should one man resist? What is he that he should make a fuss because he loses a few minutes, or is taxed too highly? The sense of the immense multitude around him presses down the individual; and, after all, he reflects, "things will come out right" in the end.

It is hard adequately to convey the impression which the vastness of the country and the swift growth of its population make upon the European visitor. I well remember how it once came on me after climbing a high mountain in an Eastern State. All around was thick forest; but the setting sun lit up peaks sixty or seventy miles away, and flashed here and there on the windings of some river past a town so far off as to seem only a spot of white. I opened my map, a large map, which I had to spread upon the rocks to examine, and tried to make out, as one would have done in Scotland or

Switzerland, the points in the view. The map, however, was useless, because the whole area of the landscape beneath me covered only two or three square inches upon it. From such a height in Scotland the eye would have ranged from sea to sea. But here when one tried to reckon how many more equally wide stretches of landscape lay between this peak and the Mississippi, which is itself only a third of the way across the continent, the calculation seemed endless and was soon abandoned. Many an Englishman comes by middle life to know nearly all England like a glove. He has travelled on all the great railroads; there is hardly a large town in which he has not acquaintances, hardly a county whose scenery is not familiar to him. But no American can be familiar with more than a small part of his country, for his country is a continent. And all Americans live their life through under the sense of this prodigious and daily growing multitude around them, which seems vaster the more you travel, and the more you realize its uniformity.

We need not here inquire whether the fatalistic attitude I have sought to sketch is the source of more good or evil. It seems at any rate inevitable: nor does it fail to produce a sort of pleasure, for what the individual loses as an individual he seems in a measure to regain as one of the multitude. If the individual is not strong, he is at any rate as strong as any one else. His will counts for as much as any other will. He is overborne by no superiority. Most men are fitter to make part of the multitude than to strive against it. Obedience is to most sweeter than independence; the Roman Catholic Church inspires in its children a stronger affection than any form of Protestantism,

for she takes their souls in charge, and assures them that, with obedience, all will be well.

That which we are presently concerned to note is how greatly such a tendency as I have described facilitates the action of opinion as a governing power, enabling it to prevail more swiftly and more completely than in countries where men have not yet learned to regard the voice of the multitude as the voice of fate. Many submit willingly; some unwillingly, yet they submit. Rarely does any one hold out and venture to tell the great majority of his countrymen that they are wrong.

Moreover, public opinion acquires a solidity which strengthens the whole body politic. Questions on which the masses have made up their minds pass out of the region of practical discussion. Controversy is confined to minor topics, and however vehemently it may rage over these, it disturbs the great underlying matters of agreement no more than a tempest stirs the depths of the Atlantic. Public order becomes more easily maintained, because individuals and small groups have learned to submit even when they feel themselves aggrieved. The man who murmurs against the world, who continues to preach a hopeless cause, incurs contempt, and is apt to be treated as a sort of lunatic. He who is too wise to murmur and too proud to go on preaching to unheeding ears comes to think that if his doctrine is true, yet the time is not ripe for it. He may be in error; but if he is right, the world will ultimately see that he is right even without his effort. One way or another he finds it hard to believe that this vast mass and force of popular thought in which he lives and moves can be ultimately wrong.

D. H. Lawrence: NEGATIVE FREEDOM

D. H. Lawrence was not a trained social analyst. His Studies in Classic American Literature, *begun in 1915 and published in 1922, makes no pretense at scholarly detachment. Lawrence despised the notion. But the power of his perception, let alone his prose, has made this work, despite its fury, one that serious students of the American character simply cannot dismiss.*

LET US LOOK at this American artist first. How did he ever get to America, to start with? Why isn't he a European still, like his father before him?

Now listen to me, don't listen to him. He'll tell you the lie you expect. Which is partly your fault for expecting it.

He didn't come in search of freedom of worship. England had more freedom of worship in the year 1700 than America had. Won by Englishmen who wanted freedom, and so stopped at home and fought for it. And got it. Freedom of worship? Read the history of New England during the first century of its existence.

Freedom anyhow? The land of the free! This the land of the free! Why, if I say anything that displeases them, the free mob will lynch me, and that's my freedom. Free? Why I have never been in any country where the individual has such an abject fear of his fellow countrymen. Because, as I say, they are free to lynch him the moment he shows he is not one of them.

No, no, if you're so fond of the truth about Queen Victoria, try a little about yourself.

Those Pilgrim Fathers and their successors never came here for freedom of worship. What did they set up when they got here? Freedom, would you call it?

They didn't come for freedom. Or if they did, they sadly went back on themselves.

All right then, what did they come for? For lots of reasons. Perhaps least of all in search of freedom of any sort: positive freedom, that is.

They came largely to get *away* — that most simple of motives. To get away. Away from what? In the long run, away from themselves. Away from everything. That's why most people have come to America, and still do come. To get away from everything they are and have been.

"Henceforth be masterless."

Which is all very well, but it isn't freedom. Rather the reverse. A hopeless sort of constraint. It is never freedom till you find something you really *positively want to be*. And people in America have always been shouting about the things they are *not*. Unless of course they are millionaires, made or in the making.

And after all there is a positive side to the movement. All that vast flood of human life that has flowed over the Atlantic in ships from Europe to America has not flowed over simply on a tide of revulsion from Europe and from the confinements of the European ways of life. This revulsion was, and still is, I believe, the prime motive in emigration. But there was some cause, even for the revulsion.

It seems as if at times man had a frenzy

for getting away from any control of any sort. In Europe the old Christianity was the real master. The Church and the true aristocracy bore the responsibility for the working out of the Christian ideals, a little irregularly, maybe, but responsible nevertheless.

Mastery, kingship, fatherhood had their power destroyed at the time of the Renaissance.

And it was precisely at this moment that the great drift over the Atlantic started. What were men drifting away from? The old authority of Europe? Were they breaking the bonds of authority, and escaping to a new more absolute unrestrainedness? Maybe. But there was more to it.

Liberty is all very well, but men cannot live without masters. There is always a master. And men either live in glad obedience to the master they believe in, or they live in a frictional opposition to the master they wish to undermine. In America this frictional opposition has been the vital factor. It has given the Yankee his kick. Only the continual influx of more servile Europeans has provided America with an obedient labouring class. The true obedience never outlasting the first generation.

But there sits the old master, over in Europe. Like a parent. Somewhere deep in every American heart lies a rebellion against the old parenthood of Europe. Yet no American feels he has completely escaped its mastery. Hence the slow, smouldering patience of American opposition. The slow, smouldering, corrosive obedience to the old master Europe, the unwilling subject, the unremitting opposition.

Whatever else you are, be masterless.

Ca Ca Caliban
Get a new master, be a new man.

Escaped slaves, we might say, people the republics of Liberia or Haiti. Liberia enough! Are we to look at America in the same way? A vast republic of escaped slaves. When you consider the hordes from eastern Europe, you might well say it: a vast republic of escaped slaves. But one dare not say this of the Pilgrim Fathers, and the great old body of idealist Americans, the modern Americans tortured with thought. A vast republic of escaped slaves. Look out, America! And a minority of earnest, self-tortured people.

The masterless.

Ca Ca Caliban
Get a new master, be a new man.

What did the Pilgrim Fathers come for, then, when they came so gruesomely over the black seas? Oh, it was in a black spirit. A black revulsion from Europe, from the old authority of Europe, from kings and bishops and popes. And more. When you look into it, more. They were black, masterful men, they wanted something else. No kings, no bishops maybe. Even no God Almighty. But also, no more of this new "humanity" which followed the Renaissance. None of this new liberty which was to be so pretty in Europe. Something grimmer, by no means free-and-easy.

America has never been easy, and is not easy to-day. Americans have always been at a certain tension. Their liberty is a thing of sheer will, sheer tension: a liberty of THOU SHALT NOT. And it has been so from the first. The land of THOU SHALT NOT. Only the first commandment is: THOU SHALT NOT PRESUME TO BE A MASTER. Hence democracy.

"We are the masterless." That is what the American Eagle shrieks. It's a Hen-Eagle.

The Spaniards refused the post-Renaissance liberty of Europe. And the Spaniards filled most of America. The Yankees, too, refused, refused the post-Renaissance humanism of Europe. First and foremost, they hated masters. But under that, they hated the flowing ease of humour in Europe. At the bottom of the American soul was always a dark suspense, at the bottom of the Spanish-American soul the same. And this dark suspense hated and hates the old European spontaneity, watches it collapse with satisfaction.

Every continent has its own great spirit of place. Every people is polarized in some particular locality, which is home, the homeland. Different places on the face of the earth have different vital effluence, different vibration, different chemical exhalation, different polarity with different stars: call it what you like. But the spirit of place is a great reality. The Nile valley produced not only the corn, but the terrific religions of Egypt. China produces the Chinese, and will go on doing so. The Chinese in San Francisco will in time cease to be Chinese, for America is a great melting pot.

There was a tremendous polarity in Italy, in the city of Rome. And this seems to have died. For even places die. The Island of Great Britain had a wonderful terrestrial magnetism or polarity of its own, which made the British people. For the moment, this polarity seems to be breaking. Can England die? And what if England dies?

Men are less free than they imagine; ah, far less free. The freest are perhaps least free.

Men are free when they are in a living homeland, not when they are straying and breaking away. Men are free when they are obeying some deep, inward voice of religious belief. Obeying from within. Men are free when they belong to a living, organic, *believing* community, active in fulfilling some unfulfilled, perhaps unrealized purpose. Not when they are escaping to some wild west. The most unfree souls go west, and shout of freedom. Men are freest when they are most unconscious of freedom. The shout is a rattling of chains, always was.

Men are not free when they are doing just what they like. The moment you can do just what you like, there is nothing you care about doing. Men are only free when they are doing what the deepest self likes.

And there is getting down to the deepest self! It takes some diving.

Because the deepest self is way down, and the conscious self is an obstinate monkey. But of one thing we may be sure. If one wants to be free, one has to give up the illusion of doing what one likes, and seek what IT wishes done.

But before you can do what IT likes, you must first break the spell of the old mastery, the old IT.

Perhaps at the Renaissance, when kingship and fatherhood fell, Europe drifted into a very dangerous half-truth: of liberty and equality. Perhaps the men who went to America felt this, and so repudiated the old world altogether. Went one better than Europe. Liberty in America has meant so far the breaking away from *all* dominion. The true liberty will only begin when Americans discover IT, and proceed possibly to fulfil IT. IT being the deepest *whole* self of man, the self in its wholeness, not idealistic halfness.

That's why the Pilgrim Fathers came to America, then; and that's why we come. Driven by IT. We cannot see that invisible winds carry us, as they carry swarms of locusts, that invisible magnetism brings us as it brings the migrating birds to their unforeknown goal. But it is so. We are not the marvellous choosers and deciders we think we are. IT chooses for us, and decides for us. Unless of course we are just escaped slaves, vulgarly cocksure of our ready-made destiny. But if we are living people, in touch with the source, IT drives us and decides us. We are free only so long as we obey. When we run counter, and think we will do as we like, we just flee around like Orestes pursued by the Eumenides.

And still, when the great day begins, when Americans have at last discovered America and their own wholeness, still there will be the vast number of escaped slaves to reckon with, those who have no cocksure, ready-made destinies.

Which will win in America, the escaped slaves, or the new whole men?

The real American day hasn't begun yet. Or at least, not yet sunrise. So far it has been the false dawn. That is, in the progressive American consciousness there has been the one dominant desire, to do away with the old thing. Do away with masters, exalt the will of the people. The will of the people being nothing but a figment, the exalting doesn't count for much. So, in the name of the will of the people, get rid of masters. When you have got rid of masters, you are left with this mere phrase of the will of the people. Then you pause and bethink yourself, and try to recover your own wholeness.

So much for the conscious American motive, and for democracy over here. Democracy in America is just the tool with which the old mastery of Europe, the European spirit, is undermined. Europe destroyed, potentially, American democracy will evaporate. America will begin.

American consciousness has so far been a false dawn. The negative ideal of democracy. But underneath, and contrary to this open ideal, the first hints and revelations of it. IT, the American whole soul.

You have got to pull the democratic and idealistic clothes off American utterance, and see what you can of the dusky body of IT underneath.

"Henceforth be masterless."

Henceforth be mastered.

IV: RECENT CONCEPTIONS: HAS THE AMERICAN CHARACTER CHANGED?

David Riesman: FROM INNER-DIRECTION TO OTHER-DIRECTION

The terminology of David Riesman's The Lonely Crowd *has entered into the vocabulary of most educated Americans, whether or not they have read the book. Everyone knows that nineteenth-century Americans were individualists (inner-directed) and that twentieth-century Americans — oneself excluded, of course — are conformists (other-directed). Such a summary statement does not do justice to Riesman's more sophisticated and complex contentions, and he most certainly would deny that he ever said anything of the kind. But after all disclaimers, his thesis does boil down to something approaching that view.*

No social analysis in the last fifteen years can match the enormous influence which The Lonely Crowd *(whose central argument is restated in the essay below) has exerted. Only recently has Riesman's thesis been significantly challenged. The question was first raised whether nineteenth-century Americans were inner-directed and whether Americans haven't always tended toward other-direction. Travel observations similar to those which have preceded this selection may start the reader on the road to an answer to these claims. But not only has Riesman's history been assailed; his popular sociology which characterizes twentieth-century Americans as other-directed has begun to receive serious scrutiny. Selections subsequent to this one will furnish some alternative conceptions of the historical and contemporary American character — conceptions which may or may not speak more directly to the reader than do Riesman's.*

IT IS A difficult problem to attempt as in this series of lectures to link the psychological understanding of people to specific political and other social phenomena. In his paper Professor Parsons tried to show how individuals play roles in a society and how these roles within a social system may harness various types of personalities. To put it more specifically, you can get the same kind of political behavior, for instance, out of quite different human types. Although the behavior has different meanings for these people, the understanding of their differences and those different meanings may be quite irrelevant to their political and public role.

Nevertheless, and this is the topic of my discourse, it seems to me that personality does influence political behavior if we look at it in a sufficiently long-run historical view. Its influence is felt not in terms of specific behavior — in terms of explaining why somebody votes for Truman or Dewey or Wallace — but only in terms of what I like to call political style, the kind of attitude a person has towards the political cosmos: how he reacts to it, how he feels it reacting to him. If one is to speak as more than a spot-news analyst of political crisis, then he must be concerned with these long-run developments both in politics and personality.

In fact, I think there is a danger for the social scientist if he allows such a phrase as political crisis to make him try to be particularly relevant in talking about spot news, the atom bomb, or what not. Because curiously enough if the social scientist is any good he can't help being relevant. He lives in our society as a participant-observer and it is no problem for him to be relevant — he can't help it. If he isn't any good, and hence irrelevant, he is sometimes likely to compensate by grandiose ambitions; and when he tries to communicate about politics — to solve present crises — he is likely to say more about his own personality than he says about politics, ironically just because he is trying too hard to talk about politics.

That is at least my prologue for taking an excursion in this paper which will go back 100 years in American history. In this way we can take a look at the changes in American character and American political style as developing from the nineteenth century to the present. I know what I have to say is difficult, and I hope that in the discussion period the unanswered ambiguities in what I say can be brought up and threshed out.

Let me first present my dramatis personae. There are two types of character in the cast: one I call the inner-directed type and the other I call the other-directed type. And they orient themselves to the world in two political styles. I call the first, the style of the moralizers, and the second, the style of the inside-dopesters. And the scene on which these moralizers and inside-dopesters play their parts is in the changing power configurations of this country in the last decades. Naturally, the broad outlines of such a drama as this must be tentative, must be experimental.

Let me begin by describing what kind of people the inner-directeds are. In framing my character types, in trying to work with character types which have psychoanalytic depth and also historical relevance, I have focused on the problem of how conformity is assured; what these people conform to; what their society or their group in society expects of them. This, it seems to me, changes over historical time. In the nineteenth century — and still to a great extent in this century — it seems to me that conformity was assured by a mechanism which I call inner-direction, in which a person was socialized in an authoritative family group by impressive and often oppressive parents and in which he internalized his image of these parents. Freud's picture of the superego is a magnificent picture of this type. This was the typical American of the middle class of the last century, the parents and grandparents of most of us today. Some of us could still be called inner-directed.

Now, the inner-directed person is oriented early in childhood towards very clear goals in life. It may be money, fame, power, goodness, or any blend of these. And he is headed for these by the kind of intimate family socialization characteristic of his age. I like to use a metaphor to describe this mechanism. I speak of these people as gyroscopically-steered. The parents install a gyroscope in them and it stabilizes them all their life. They are less independent than they seem because the gyroscope keeps them on the course for which their parents headed them.

What is the kind of society in which such types will live and work? Theirs is a world in which the opening frontiers are the frontiers of production, discovery, science. We might call it the job-minded society — a society in which people are very much aware and interested in the malleability of the physical environment, the organizational environment, and in their social mobility, their ambitions. Their preoccupation is to harness themselves to fulfilling the tasks of the expanding society which needs a large physical plant, extensive social organization, extensive military preparation. In this kind of a job-minded society people are protected from too close resonance with each other by their concentration on these necessary and rewarding tasks.

It does not follow from this that the inner-directed man, concentrated on these tasks, is not concerned with people. People may be means to the ends of his gyroscopically-installed goal — people as voters, workers, soldiers. And he may be a pretty good manipulator of them for these ends. The point that is decisive in distinguishing him from the other-directed man is that he does not need anything from these peoples as ends in themselves. He does not look to them for approval. He does not look to them for warmth. He looks to them for usefulness and in other more specific and more tangible ways.

Obviously I am speaking in terms of contrast, and in order to do so I create what those who have sociological training would recognize as an ideal type — ideal not in the sense of noble, but ideal in the sense of abstract. There is no pure inner-directed man. Most of us are blends. We can make a judgment of the emphasis of these tendencies within given individuals or given social epochs.

In this job-minded society in which people orient themselves early towards clearly defined goals, young people had clear models to follow. They might be very ambitious and hitch themselves to some star in the ancestral firmament. If they were going to be scientists, they might want to imitate Pasteur; or if painters, they might want to imitate Renoir. They thought in terms of great men. Maybe they thought their parents were great men; and they headed for that. They modeled themselves on these people. This was possible because the personal star developed in this way did not become obsolete but was good for a lifetime. In the case of the personality market, the market on which people sell themselves, there was a fair amount of stability so that a person who decided, when he was very young, that he wanted to be like, let us say, Henry Ford or Abraham Lincoln was not likely to find people calling him quaint by the time he was fifty — because others had gyroscopes too, spinning at about the same pace, moving in the same direction. People who had this type of character found themselves on the whole rewarded, found their lives unproblematical in the sense of concern with whether they fitted or not. To put the matter more generally, there was a certain fit between social structure and character structure.

Having said this, I think I have to stop at once and suggest that one should not get nostalgic about "life with father." As a play it may be amusing; but if he is your father, if he has hurt you, that may be a different matter. I think this nostalgia is actually an important social and political force in our time, and I want to come back to it later on.

Let me now introduce the next person in the dramatis personae, the other-directed. A new source of conformity is required, it seems to me, for the urban upper middle class in our big cities, a conformity for which gyroscopic adaption is not sufficiently flexible, not sufficiently resonant with other people. And for this new source of conformity I like to use the metaphor of the radar set. The other-directed child has a radar set installed, by which he can understand the interpersonal environment and see its signals around him. He is oriented very early in life, not to his ancestors, not to his parents or to his image of their exalted selves, but to his peers; that is, the other kids on the block, the other kids at school, the people who will do a great deal of the job of socializing him. In fact, those who are familiar with the work of Harry Stack Sullivan can see that he has become in a sense the analyst of this age because he was the person above all others who called attention to the importance of the peer group in the process of socialization.

One can see that the parents play a hand in this by their concern with whether the child is popular, how he is getting along with the other kids. One can see that the school also is concerned today more with morale than with morality — concerned with the social atmosphere. I speak now obviously of the progressive schools in the suburban and urban areas where the other-directed as a character type is emerging. The school puts a youngster in with the five-year-olds to see if he fits with the five-year-olds, not in terms of how much he knows,

but in terms of how he gets along. And the parents are anxious and judge their success with their children by how the children get along, how popular they are; the parents act as chauffeurs and managers for the continuous stage performance of their children in the peer group.

It is important to see what the radar brings to the other-directed child. It brings direction; it brings a sense of what is worth having in life, what is worth experiencing, what is worth talking about, thinking about. And the goals obviously change with what the radar senses rather than being set for a lifetime as in the earlier epoch. Obviously I don't mean to imply that parents set about consciously to create little paragons who will fit into the society of 1950 or 1960 or 1970. They aren't that calculating, even if they would like to be. It is a long and complicated story and one, I am sure, many social investigators have worked on and thought about: how it happens that the parents, without actually being consciously aware of their role in this process, produce the children whom the next society makes use of. It is a story I cannot go into here. But I want to remark on just one of the changes from inner-direction to other-direction which might be called the change from bringing up children to bringing up father, for children may bring up parents in the other-directed society.

I think one might recognize, if he is interested in historical questions, that this does not sound so new. Perhaps the other-directed American is in a way the American as he appeared to the eyes of 150 years of European observation. The European always thought that the American was a person who cared more for what his fellows thought than anything else, that the American was more concerned with indiscriminate approval and with warmth, more dependent on his neighbors than the European was — or at least more than the European who came to America to look around. And certainly there is very much in the way of social change and so on which helps to explain why it is we have a comic strip called "Bringing Up Father" in which the daughter as well as the mother cooperates.

Now, what is the kind of society in which the other-directed person moves? For him the frontiers are not the frontiers of production but the frontiers of consumption, the frontiers of much more abundant leisure and consumer goods. He moves in a society where — at least in his picture of it — the main productive job is done. The steel mills are built, the railroads are built, the mines are dug, the government organizations are set up. And his concern is to live as a consumer. Those who may be economists can recognize the touch of Keynesian economics in that. But I want to make clear that I am not talking about conspicuous consumption — I am not talking about keeping up with the Joneses. That is an older, perhaps a traditional pattern. As long as one is concerned only with what goods he is getting out of the society, out of its physical productiveness, he is still inner-directed. A person is other-directed only when his interest is not in the goods — he takes those for granted. After all, the middle-class family can have a car, a mink coat, good food, and so on. Consumption itself is no issue for most of these people. The problem for the other-directed person is not the goods themselves, but the right attitudes about the goods. Is he having the right experiences vis-à-vis the wine he drinks, the car he drives, the girl he sleeps with, and so on? That is the problem. And he looks to others for guidance as to whether he is experiencing the right experiences on the frontiers of consumption. He takes more or less for granted that he has the wherewithal, the ability to pay unremittingly to provide himself with the goods themselves.

This is another way of saying that in America we have moved from a job-minded society to a people-minded society in which one's concern is no longer with the malleability of the materiel but with the malleability of the personnel. It is a society in which people are no longer protected from each other by the objectivity of their workaday tasks and in which response from others becomes an end in life as well as a means.

In fact, I think it is quite interesting to look at specific individuals and see to what extent they may rationalize their need for warmth, their need for approval from others, in terms of, let us say, some sensible and easily rationalized goal such as money or security.

Think of Willy Loman, in the play, *Death of a Salesman,* as a man who looked to selling, not primarily for money — that too — but as a source of affection, a means of justifying himself, a *Weltanschauung* — all these things wrapped up in the job of the salesman. Incidentally, the play seemed quite incomprehensible to Londoners. They couldn't understand why anybody was that interested in selling and why people responded in terms other than cash. The English response showed that they didn't understand Americans. Obviously in such a society the old clear goals of ambition, the old stars of the heavenly firmament by which the inner-directed man guided himself no longer guide people.

Let me give an illustration. There was an interview with a thirteen-year-old girl about her comic-reading habits. She was asked what comics she preferred and she said Superman. Then she was asked why. "Oh, Superman can fly," she said, "and flying is very important." "Would you like to be able to fly?" the interviewer asked. "Oh, no, that would be kind of conspicuous," the girl said. Here one sees the fear of being conspicuous, the fear of being too ambitious, the fear somebody might say, "So you think you're big — so you think you're something." These are the fears which make it hard for people brought up in other-directed circles to have the same kind of sometimes fanatical and crushing ambition which was a characteristic of the middle-class man of an earlier epoch, a characteristic which still hangs on in this country because — obviously I am talking about trends — there are still men like Henry Ford.

I am talking about something that the investigator finds more among the young than the old, more in the upper middle class in the very large metropolitan areas than in the smaller cities and smaller towns. And this seems to me to be connected in subtle ways with the alteration of mobility channels. One no longer gets ahead in the society by making a better mousetrap but by packaging an old mousetrap in a new way and selling it by selling one's self first.

Those who know Erich Fromm's book *Man for Himself* will recognize the similarity of his marketing orientation to what I call the other-directed man. The man of the marketing orientation is concerned with how he is doing on the personality market of the large corporate enterprises, private, public, academic, and what not, of our society. And in order to succeed on the personality market he must be different but not too different; as different as Ford from Chevrolet — maybe as far different as Studebaker from Ford. And so he must always use his radar to find out: "Am I different enough to be recognized — to have a brand name, so to speak, for my personality — but not so different that I will be priced out of the market as an eccentric?" But even eccentricity can be made to pay in the right professions. Success comes in our society increasingly, it seems to me, through a person's ability to be malleable enough to fit into a cooperative network.

Adam Smith used the phrase "the invisible hand" to describe the economic organization of the free market. I think we have moved from the invisible hand to the glad hand and that today people in industry and the professions — particularly in medicine — are engaged in a cooperative network in which the esteem of colleagues is decisive for one's fate and in which to be known as a ratebuster would exclude one from the system. To be sure, there are survivals of the older age, but I am talking of the social character that seems to me to be emerging.

Daniel Bell: AMERICA AS A MASS SOCIETY: A CRITIQUE

Daniel Bell, like Riesman, teaches sociology (Bell at Columbia, Riesman at Harvard), and came to do so relatively late in his career life. Riesman was a lawyer and Bell was an editor of The New Leader *and then* Fortune Magazine. *Possibly, the experience of working for these two very different magazines taught him how to expose the slippery relationship between theories of mass society and the institutional realities which they seem to describe. In the following essay from* The End of Ideology, *he closely and critically examines the fundamental and oft-repeated assumptions of Riesman and other more philosophical authors who write of modern America and Europe as mass societies filled with lonely, faceless crowds.*

THE SENSE of a radical dehumanization of life which has accompanied events of the past few decades has given rise to the theory of "mass society." One can say that, Marxism apart, it is probably the most influential social theory in the Western world today. While no single individual has stamped his name on it — to the extent that Marx is associated with the transformation of personal relations under capitalism into commodity values, or Freud with the role of the irrational and unconscious in behavior — the theory is central to the thinking of the principal aristocrat, Catholic, or Existentialist critics of modern society. These critics — Ortega y Gasset, Paul Tillich, Karl Jaspers, Gabriel Marcel, Emil Lederer, Hannah Arendt, and others — have been concerned less with the general conditions of freedom in society than with the freedom of the *person* and with the possibility, for some few persons, of achieving a sense of individual self in our mechanized society. And this is the source of their appeal.

The conception of the "mass society" can be summarized as follows: The revolutions in transport and communications have brought men into closer contact with each other and bound them in new ways; the division of labor has made them more interdependent; tremors in one part of society affect all others. Despite this greater interdependence, however, individuals have grown more estranged from one another. The old primary group ties of family and local community have been shattered; ancient parochial faiths are questioned; few unifying values have taken their place. Most important, the critical standards of an educated elite no longer shape opinion or taste. As a result, mores and morals are in constant flux, relations between individuals are tangential or compartmentalized, rather than organic. At the same time, greater mobility, spatial and social, intensifies concern over status. Instead of a fixed or known status, symbolized by dress or title, each person assumes a multiplicity of roles and constantly has to prove himself in a succession of new situations. Because of all this, the individual loses a coherent sense of self. His anxieties increase. There ensues a search for new faiths. The stage is thus set for the charismatic leader, the secular messiah, who, by bestowing upon each person the semblance of necessary grace and of fullness of personality, supplies a substitute for the older unifying belief that the mass society has destroyed.

In a world of lonely crowds seeking individual distinction, where values are constantly translated into economic calculabilities, where in extreme situations shame and conscience can no longer restrain the most dreadful excesses of terror, the theory of the mass society seems a forceful, realistic description of contemporary society, an accurate reflection of the *quality* and *feeling* of modern life. But when one seeks to apply the theory of mass society, analytically, it becomes very slippery. Ideal types, like the shadows in Plato's cave, generally never give us more than a silhouette. So, too, with the theory of "mass society." Each of the statements making up the theory, as set forth in the second paragraph above, might be true, but they do not follow necessarily from one another. Nor can we say that all the conditions described are present at any one time or place. More than that, there is no organizing principle — other than the general concept of a "break-down of values" — that puts the individual elements of theory together in a logical, meaningful — let alone historical — manner. And when we examine the way the "theory" is used by those who employ it, we find ourselves even more at a loss.

In trying to sort out the ambiguities in the use of the phrase, we can distinguish perhaps five different, and sometimes contradictory, usages:

1. *Mass as undifferentiated number.* As commonly used in the term "mass media," "mass" implies that standardized material is transmitted to "all groups of the population uniformly." As understood generally by sociologists, a *mass* is a heterogeneous and undifferentiated audience, as opposed to a *class,* or any parochial and relatively homogeneous segment. Some sociologists have been tempted to go further and make "mass" a rather pejorative term. Because the mass media subject a diverse audience to a common set of cultural materials, it is argued that these experiences must necessarily lie outside the personal — and therefore meaningful — experiences to which the individual responds directly. A movie audience, for example, is a "mass" because the individuals looking at the screen are, in the words of the American sociologist Herbert Blumer, "separate, detached and anonymous." The mass "has no social organization, no

body of custom and tradition, no established set of rules or rituals, no organized group of sentiments, no structure of status roles and no established leadership."

To become part of the mass is to be divorced — or "alienated" — from oneself. And the instruments which project the dominant social values that men (and women and children) choose as their *imago,* or ideal image and desire — television, radio, and the movies — impose a mass response on their audience.

2. *Mass as the judgment by the incompetent.* As first introduced by the late Ortega y Gasset in 1931, in his famous *Revolt of the Masses,* the terms "masses" and "mass" had a far different meaning than the usage implied by the term "mass media" and its invidious connotations. For Ortega, the word "mass" did not designate a group of persons — the masses were not the workers, even though the revolutionary movements of the time had equated the two — but the low *quality* of modern civilization, resulting from the loss of a commanding position by the "gentlemen" who once made up the educated elite. Modern taste, for Ortega, represents the judgment of the unqualified. Modern life "makes a *tabula rasa* of all classicism." Nothing that is in the past can be "any possible model or standard." Even "the famous Renaissance reveals itself as a period of narrow provincialism — why not use the word? — ordinary." Modern culture, since it disowns the past, seeks a "free expression of its vital desires"; it becomes, therefore, an unrestrained "spoiled child" with no controlling standards, "no limit to its caprice." In Ortega, one finds the most sweeping attack against all "modernity." His is the disdain of the humanist for the vulgar.

3. *Mass as the mechanized society.* In German romanticism, in its idealization

of nature and the pastoral, one finds the source of much of the protest against modern life. For these writers — and the poets and critics Ernst and Friedrich George Juenger can be taken as typical — the dehumanizing element is technology. The mass society is a mechanical society. Society has become an "apparatus." The machine impresses its style on man, makes life mathematical and precise; existence takes on a masklike character: the steel helmet and the welder's face-guard symbolize the individual's disappearance into his technical function. The regulated, functional man emerges as a new type, hard and ruthless, a cog in the technological press.

4. *The mass as the bureaucratized society.* Less romantic, but equally critical, are those theorists who seek extreme rationalization and extreme bureaucratization — the *over-organization* of life — as the salient features of the mass society. The idea of "rationalization" goes back to Hegel and Marx and along with it the notions of "estrangement" or "alienation," "reification," and the "fetishism of commodities" — all of which express the thought that in modern society man has become a "thing," an object manipulated by society, rather than a subject who can remake life in accordance with his own desires. In our time, Georg Simmel, Max Weber, and Karl Mannheim have developed and elaborated these concepts. In Mannheim's work — notably in his *Man and Society in an Age of Reconstruction* — the diverse strands are all brought together.

Mannheim's argument, put schematically, runs as follows: modern large-scale organization, oriented exclusively to efficiency, creates hierarchies that concentrate all decisions at the top. Even technical decisions are removed from the shop floor and centered in specialized bodies that have no direct contact with work. Since the concern is solely with efficiency, rather than human satisfactions, all solutions to problems are defined in relation to this single value. Mannheim calls this "functional rationality," or direct means-ends relationships, in contrast to "substantial rationality," which is the application of Reason to human affairs.

This concentration of decision-making not only creates conformity but stunts the initiative of subordinates and leaves them unsatisfied in their personal needs for gratification and esteem. (In effect, the demand for submission to extreme rationality deprives the individual of the power to act rationally; i.e., in accordance with reason. This frustration seeks release in irrational ways.) Normally, the routinization of one's job dulls the edge of frustration and provides some security. But when unemployment looms, the helplessness becomes sharpened, and self-esteem is threatened. Since individuals cannot rationally locate the source of their frustration (i.e., the impersonal bureaucratic system itself), they will, under these circumstances, seek scapegoats and turn to fascism.

5. *The mass as mob.* While for Mannheim, and the neo-Marxists, mass society is equated with monolithic bureaucratization, for Emil Lederer and Hannah Arendt it is defined by the elimination of difference, by uniformity, aimlessness, alienation, and the failure of integration.

In Lederer's view, society is made up of many social groups united by function or self-interest, some rational in purpose, some irrational. So long as society is stratified, these groups can impose only partial control, and irrational emotions are restricted. But when the lines dividing social groups break down, the people become volatile and febrile "masses," ready to be manipulated by a leader.

Hannah Arendt, perhaps because she writes a decade later, sees the masses as already overspilling the bounds. The masses are those who, because of indifference or simply sheer number, do not belong to "political parties or municipal government or professional organizations or trade-unions" — in short, organizations that exist to satisfy a common interest — and they "form the majority of those large numbers of neutral, politically indifferent people who never join a party or hardly ever go to the polls."

Such people already stand "outside" of society. The revolt of the masses is a revolt against the "loss of social status along with which [is] lost the whole sector of communal relationships in whose framework common sense makes sense. . . . The masses [become] obsessed by a desire to escape from reality because in their essential homelessness they can no longer bear its accidental incomprehensible aspects."

And so, because modern life sunders all social bonds, and because the techniques of modern communication have perfected the means whereby propaganda can manipulate the masses, the "age of the masses" is now upon us.

What strikes one first about these varied uses of the concept of mass society is how little they reflect or relate to the complex, richly striated social relations of the real world. Take Blumer's example of the movie audience as "separate, detached, and anonymous." Presumably, a large number of individuals, because they have been subjected to similar experiences, now share some common psychological reality in which the differences between individual and individual become blurred; accordingly we get the sociological assumption that each person is now of "equal weight," and therefore

a sampling of what such disparate individuals say they think constitutes "*mass* opinion." But is this so? Individuals are not *tabulae rasae*. They bring varying social conceptions to the same experience and go away with dissimilar responses They may be silent, separate, detached, and anonymous while watching the movie, but afterwards they talk about it with friends and exchange opinions and judgments. They are once again members of particular social groups. Would one say that several hundred or a thousand individuals home alone at night, but all reading the same book, constitute a "mass"?

Because romantic feeling colors critical judgment, the attacks on modern life often have an unduly strong emotional charge. The image of "facelessness," for example, is given a metaphysical twist by Gabriel Marcel: "The individual, in order to belong to the mass . . . has had to . . . divest himself of that substantial reality which was linked to his initial individuality. . . . The incredibly sinister role of the press, the cinema, the radio has consisted in passing that original reality through a pair of flattening rollers to substitute for it a super-imposed pattern of ideas, an image with no real roots in the deep being of the subject of this experiment." Perhaps terms like "original reality" and "real roots in the deep being" have a meaning that escapes an empiricist temper, but without the press, the radio, etc., etc. — and they are not monolithic — in what way, short of being everywhere at once, can one learn of events that take place elsewhere? Or should one go back to the happy ignorance of earlier days?

Some of the images of life in the mass society, as presented by its critics, border on caricature. According to Ernst Juenger, traffic demands traffic regulations, and so the public becomes conditioned to automatism. Karl Jaspers has written that in the "technical mass order" the home is transformed "into a lair or sleeping place." Even more puzzling is the complaint against modern medicine. "In medical practice . . . patients are now dealt with in the mass according to the principle of rationalization, being sent to institutes for technical treatment, the sick being classified in groups and referred to this or that specialized department. . . . The supposition is that, like everything else, medical treatment has become a sort of manufactured article."

The attack on the mass society sometimes widens into an attack on science itself. For Ortega, "the scientific man is the prototype of the mass-man," because science, by encouraging specialization, has made the scientist "hermetic and self-satisfied within his limitations." Ortega draws from this the sweeping conclusion that "the most immediate result of this unbalanced specialization has been that today, when there are more 'scientists' than ever, there are much less 'cultured' men than, for example, about 1750." But how is one to verify such a comparison between 1750 and the present? Even if we could establish comparable categories, surely Ortega would have been the first to shy away from statistical comparisons. Moreover, can we assume that because a man specializes in his work, he is unable, in his leisure and in reflection, to appreciate culture? And what is "culture"? Would not Ortega admit that we have more knowledge of the world than in 1750 — knowledge not only of nature but of the inner life of man? Is knowledge to be divorced from culture, or is "true culture" a narrow area of classical learning in which eternal truths reside?

One could argue, of course, that reading a book, to cite my previous example, is a qualitatively different experience

from going to a movie. But this leads precisely to the first damaging ambiguity in the theory of the mass society. Two things are mixed up in that theory: a judgment regarding the *quality* of modern experience — with much of which any sensitive individual might agree — and a presumed scientific statement concerning the disorganization of society created by industrialization and by the demand of the masses for equality. It is the second of these statements with which this essay quarrels.

Behind the theory of social disorganization lies a romantic — and somewhat false — notion of the past, which sees society as having once been made up of small, "organic," close-knit communities (called *Gemeinschaften* in the terminology of the sociologists) that were shattered by industrialism and modern life, and replaced by a large, impersonal, "atomistic" society (called *Gesellschaft*) that is unable to provide the basic gratifications, and call forth the loyalties, that the older communities knew. These distinctions are, however, completely riddled by value judgments. Everyone is against atomism and for "organic living." But if we substitute, with good logic, the term "total" for "organic," and "individualistic" for "atomistic," the whole argument looks quite different. In any case, a great weakness in the theory is its lack of history-mindedness. The transition to a mass society, if it be such, was not effected suddenly, explosively, within a single lifetime, but took generations to mature. In its sociological determinism, the hypothesis overlooks the human capacity for adaptiveness and creativeness, for ingenuity in shaping new social forms. Such new forms may be trade unions whose leaders rise from the ranks — there are 50,000 trade-union locals in this country that form little worlds of their own — or the persistence under new conditions of ethnic groups and solidarities.

But more than mere contradictions in usage, ambiguities in terminology, and a lack of historical sense are involved in the theory of the mass society. It is at heart a defense of an aristocratic cultural tradition — a tradition that does carry with it an important but neglected conception of liberty — and a doubt that the large mass of mankind can ever become truly educated or acquire an appreciation of culture. Thus, the theory often becomes a conservative defense of privilege. This defense is at times so extreme as to pose a conflict between "culture" and "social justice." The argument (reminiscent of the title of Matthew Arnold's book *Culture and Anarchy*) is made that any attempts of social betterment must harm culture. And, while mainly directed against "bourgeois" society, the theory also strikes at radicalism and its egalitarian notions.

The fear of the "mass" has its roots in the dominant conservative tradition of Western political thought, which in large measure still shapes many of the political and sociological categories of social theory — i.e., in authoritarian definitions of leadership and in the image of the "mindless masses." The picture of the "mass" as capable only of violence and excess originates with Aristotle's *Politics*. In his threefold typology, democracy is equated with the rule of *hoi polloi* — who are easily swayed by demagogues — and which must degenerate into tyranny. This notion of the masses, developed in Hellenistic times, was deepened by the struggles between plebes and aristocracy in the Roman republic, and by the efforts of the Caesars to exploit mob support; and the image of the insensate mob fed by "bread and circuses" became deeply imprinted on history. (From Plutarch, for example, came the description of the fickle masses and the wily tribunes that was drawn upon so directly by Shakespeare in his tragedy *Coriolanus*.) Early Christian theory justified its fear of the masses with a theory about human nature. In the religious terms of Augustine — as, later, in the secularized version of Hobbes — the Earthly City bore an ineradicable stain of blood: in Paradise there was neither private property nor government; property and police were the consequence of the Fall of Man; property and police were signs, therefore, not of man's civilization but of his corruption; they were necessary means of keeping man in check.

But it was the French Revolution that transplanted the image of the "mindless masses" into modern consciousness. The destruction of the *ancien régime* and the rallying cry of "equality" sharpened the fear of conservative, and especially Catholic, critics that traditional values (meaning political, social, and religious dogma) would be destroyed. For a Tocqueville and an Acton, there was an irreducible conflict between liberty and equality; liberty guaranteed each man the right to be different, whereas equality meant a "leveling" of tastes to the lowest common denominator. For a Max Scheler, as well as an Ortega, the mass society meant a "democracy of the emotions," which could unleash only irrational forces. For the Catholic de Maistre, as for the Anglican T. S. Eliot, the equality of men meant the destruction of the harmony and authority so necessary to a healthy, integrated society. From this traditionalist point of view, Nazism has been characterized not as a reaction against, but the inevitable end-product of, democracy. Hitler is seen as a replica of the classical demagogue swaying the mindless masses and leading them in nihilistic revolt against the traditional culture of Europe.

Important as these conceptions are, as reminders of the meaning of liberty, and of excellence, they reflect a narrow conception of human potentialities. The question of social change has to be seen against the large political canvas. The starting point of modern politics, as Karl Mannheim has pointed out, came after the Reformation, when chiliasm, or religiously inspired millennial striving to bring about heaven on earth, became an expression of the demands for social and economic betterment of the lower strata of society. Blind resentment of things as they were was thereby given principle, reason, and eschatological force, and directed to definite political goals. The equality of all souls became the equality of all individuals and the right of everyone, as enlightened by progressive revelation, to make a judgment on society.

Comte, the father of modern sociology, expressed great horror at the idea of this universal right to one's own opinion. No community could exist, he wrote, unless its members had a certain degree of confidence in one another, and this, he said, was incompatible with the right of everyone to submit the very foundations of society to discussion whenever he felt like it. In calling attention to the dangers of free criticism, Comte pointed to the decline in public morals as evidenced by the increase of divorces, the effacement of traditional class distinctions, and the ensuing impudence of individual ambitions. It was part of the function of government, he thought, to prevent the diffusion of ideas and the anarchic spread of intellectual freedom.

Modern society, apparently, does not bear Comte out: though the foundations of privilege go on being challenged in the name of justice, society does not collapse. Few moralists would now uphold the bleak view once expressed by Malthus, that "from the inevitable laws of human nature some human beings will be exposed to want. These are the unhappy persons who in the great lottery of life have drawn a blank." The most salient fact about modern life — capitalist and communist — is the ideological commitment to social change. And by change is meant the striving for material, economic betterment, greater opportunity for individuals to exercise their talents, and an appreciation of culture by wider masses of people. Can any society deny these aspirations?

It is curious that in these "aristocratic" critiques of modern society, refracted as they are through the glass of an idealized feudal past, democracy is identified with equality alone. The role of constitutionalism and of the rule of law, which, with universal suffrage, are constituent elements of the Western democratic structure, are overlooked. The picture of modern culture as debauched by concessions to popular taste—a picture that leaves out the great rise in the general appreciation of culture — is equally overdrawn. If it is granted that mass society is compartmentalized, superficial in personal relations, anonymous, transitory, specialized, utilitarian, competitive, acquisitive, mobile, and status-hungry, the obverse side of the coin must be shown, too — the right to privacy, to free choice of friends and occupation, status on the basis of achievement rather than of ascription, a plurality of norms and standards, rather than the exclusive and monopolistic social controls of a single dominant group. For if, as Sir Henry Maine once put it, the movement of modern society has been from status to contract, then it has been, in that light, a movement from a fixed place in the world to possible freedom.

The early theorists of the mass society (Ortega, Marcel) focused attention on the "deterioration of excellence," while the later theorists (Mannheim, Lederer, Arendt) called attention to the way in which the over-organization and, at the same time, the disruption of the social fabric facilitated the rise of fascism. Recently, in the light of Communist successes, the argument has been advanced that the mass society, because it cannot provide for the individual's real participation in effective social groups, is particularly vulnerable to Communist penetration, and that the mass organization, because it is so unwieldy, is peculiarly susceptible to Communist penetration and manipulation. Certainly, the Communists have scored enormous successes in infiltration, and their "front organization" may be counted as one of the great political inventions of our century. But without discounting Communist techniques, the real problem here lies less with the "mass society" as such (aside from the excuse it affords disaffected intellectuals for attacks on modern culture) than with the capacity or incapacity of the given social order to satisfy the demands for social mobility and higher standards of living that arise once social change is under way. This is the key to any radical appeal.

It is not poverty *per se* that leads people to revolt; poverty most often induces fatalism and despair, and a reliance, embodied in ritual and superstitious practices, on supernatural help. *Social tensions are an expression of unfulfilled expectations*. It is only when expectations are aroused that radicalism can take hold. Radical strength is greatest (and here the appeal of communism must be seen as a variant of the general appeal of radicalism) in societies where awareness of class differences runs deep, expectations of social advancement outstrip possibilities, and the establishments of culture fail to make room for aspiring intellectuals.

It is among industrial workers rather than apathetic peasants (in Milan rather than Calabria), among frustrated intellectuals rather than workers long unionized (e.g., India), that radicalism spreads. Resentment, as Max Scheler once noted, is among the most potent of human motives; it is certainly that in politics. It is in the advanced industrial countries, principally the United States, Britain, and northwestern Europe, where national income *has* been rising, where mass expectations of an equitable share in that increase are relatively fulfilled, and where social mobility affects ever greater numbers, that extremist politics have the least hold. It may be, as the late Joseph Schumpeter pessimistically believed, that in newly awakened societies, like Asia's, the impatient expectations of key social strata, particularly the intellectuals, may so exceed the actual possibilities of economic expansion that communism will come to look like the only plausible solution to the majority. Whether this will happen in India and Indonesia is one of the crucial political questions of the next decade. But at any rate it is not the mass society, but the inability, pure and simple, of any society to meet impatient popular expectations that makes for a strong response to radical appeals.

From the viewpoint of the mass-society hypothesis, the United States ought to be exceptionally vulnerable to the politics of disaffection. In our country, urbanization, industrialization, and democratization have eroded older primary and community ties on a scale unprecedented in social history. Yet, though large-scale unemployment during the depression was more prolonged and more severe here than in any country in Western Europe, the Communist movement never gained a real foothold in the United States, nor has any fascist movement on a European model arisen. How does one explain this?

It is asserted that the United States is an "atomized" society composed of lonely, isolated individuals. One forgets the truism, expressed sometimes as a jeer, that Americans are a nation of joiners. There are in the United States today at least 200,000 voluntary organizations, associations, clubs, societies, lodges, and fraternities, with an aggregate (but obviously overlapping) membership of close to 80 million men and women. In no other country in the world, probably, is there such a high degree of voluntary communal activity, expressed sometimes in absurd rituals, yet often providing real satisfactions for real needs.

"It is natural for the ordinary American," wrote Gunnar Myrdal, "when he sees something that is wrong to feel not only that there should be a law against it, but also that an organization should be formed to combat it." Some of these voluntary organizations are pressure groups — business, farm, labor, veterans, trade associations, the aged, etc. — but thousands more are like the National Association for the Advancement of Colored People, the American Civil Liberties Union, the League of Women Voters, the American Jewish Committee, the Parent-Teachers Associations, local community-improvement groups, and so on, each of which affords hundreds of individuals concrete, emotionally shared activities.

Equally astonishing are the number of ethnic group organizations in this country carrying on varied cultural, social, and political activities. The number of Irish, Italian, Jewish, Polish, Czech, Finnish, Bulgarian, Bessarabian, and other national groups, their hundreds of fraternal, communal, and political groups, each playing a role in the life of America, is staggering.

Even in urban neighborhoods, where anonymity is presumed to flourish, the extent of local ties is astounding. Within the city limits of Chicago, for example, there are 82 community newspapers with a total weekly circulation of almost one million; within Chicago's larger metropolitan area, there are 181. According to standard sociological theory, these local papers providing news and gossip about neighbors should slowly decline under the pressure of the national media. Yet the reverse is true. In Chicago, the number of such newspapers has increased 165 per cent since 1910; in those forty years, circulation has jumped 770 per cent. As sociologist Morris Janowitz, who studied these community newspapers, observed: "If society were as impersonal, as self-centered and barren as described by some who are preoccupied with the one-way trend from 'Gemeinschaft' to 'Gesellschaft' seem to believe, the levels of criminality, social disorganization and psychopathology which social science seeks to account for would have to be viewed as very low rather than (as viewed now) alarmingly high."

It may be argued that the existence of such a large network of voluntary associations says little about the cultural level of the country concerned. It may well be, as Ortega maintains, that cultural standards throughout the world have declined (in everything? — in architecture, dress, design?), but nonetheless a greater proportion of the population today participates in worthwhile cultural activities. This has been almost an inevitable concomitant of the doubling — *literally* — of the American standard of living over the last fifty years.

The rising levels of education have meant a rising appreciation of culture. In the United States, more dollars are spent on concerts of classical music than on baseball. Sales of books have doubled in a decade. There are over a thousand symphony orchestras, and several hundred museums, institutes and colleges are purchasing art in the United States today. Various other indexes can be cited to show the growth of a vast middlebrow society. And in coming years, with steadily increasing productivity and leisure, the United States will become an even more active "consumer" of culture.

It has been argued that the American mass society imposes an excessive conformity upon its members. But it is hard to discern who is conforming to what. The *New Republic* cries that "hucksters are sugarcoating the culture." The *National Review*, organ of the "radical right," raises the banner of iconoclasm against the domination of opinion-making in our society by "the liberals." *Fortune* decries the growth of "organization man." Each of these tendencies exists, yet in historical perspective there is probably less conformity to an over-all mode of conduct today than at any time within the last half century in America. True, there is less bohemianism than in the twenties (though increased sexual tolerance) and less political radicalism than in the thirties (though the New Deal enacted sweeping reforms). But does the arrival at a political dead center mean the establishment, too, of a dead norm? I do not think so. One would be hard put to find today the "conformity" *Main Street* exacted of Carol Kennicott

thirty years ago. With rising educational levels, more individuals are able to indulge a wider variety of interests. ("Twenty years ago you couldn't sell Beethoven out of New York," reports a record salesman. "Today we sell Palestrina, Monteverdi, Gabrielli, and Renaissance and Baroque music in large quantities.")

The curious fact, perhaps, is that no one in the United States defends conformity. Everyone is against it, and probably everyone always was. Thirty-five years ago you could easily rattle any middle-class American by charging him with being a "Babbitt." Today you can do so by accusing him of conformity. The problem is to know who is accusing whom. In December, 1958, the *Reader's Digest* (circulation twelve million) reprinted an article from *Woman's Day* (circulation five million) with the title, "The Danger of Being Too Well-Adjusted." The point of the article is that great men were not adjusted, and the article quotes a psychiatrist who says that "we've made conformity into a religion"; we ought to remember, however, that each child is different "and ought to be."

Such citation is no proof that there is not "conformity" in the middle class; but if there is, there is also a great deal of anxiety and finger-pointing about it. Certainly those who live on the margin of society — the Upper Bohemians, whose manners soon become the style for the culture — seek frantically to find different ways of emphasizing their non-conformity. In Hollywood, where Pickfair society in the twenties counterfeited a European monarchy (and whose homes crossed Louis XIV with Barnum & Bailey), "non-conformity," according to *Life* magazine (in its jumbo Entertainment issue of December 22, 1958 — readership twenty-five million), "is now the key to social importance and that Angry Middle-Aged man, Frank Sinatra, is its prophet and reigning social monarch." The Sinatra set, *Life* points out, deliberately mocks the old Hollywood taboos and is imitated by a host of other sets that eagerly want to be non-conformist as well. Significantly — a fact *Life* failed to mention — the reigning social set and its leaders, Sinatra, Dean Martin, Sammy Davis, Jr., are all from minority groups and from the wrong side of the tracks. Sinatra and Martin are Italian, Davis a Negro. In earlier times in American life, a minority group, having bulled its way to the top, would usually ape the style and manners of the established status community. In Hollywood, the old status hierarchies have been fragmented, the new sets celebrate their triumph by jeering at the pompous ways of the old.

At the margins of the literary life, and a different social phenomenon, are the Beatniks, a hopped-up, jazzed-up, souped-up, self-proclaimed group of outcasts who are rebelling against the "highly organized academic and literary movement employment agency of the Neoanti-reconstructionist [who form] a dense crust of custom over American cultural life." But the singular fact is, as Delmore Schwartz recently argued, that these beatniks are imaginary rebels, "since the substance of their work is a violent advocacy of a nonconformism which they already possess . . . since nonconformism of almost every variety had become acceptable and respectable and available to everyone. Unlike the Bohemianism of the past, which had to attack the dominant Puritanism and Victorianism of respectable society in a variety of forms, including the censorship of books, Prohibition and a prudery enforced by the police, the new nonconformism has no

genuine enemy . . . hence the new rebel bears a great deal of resemblance to a prize fighter trying to knock out an antagonist who is not in the ring with him." The additional sardonic fact is that the man in the gray flannel suit, the presumed target of the Beatniks, is, as Russell Lynes pointed out, especially if he is in advertising, or the entertainment media, an Upper Bohemian himself. The job is accepted as a means of obtaining an income in order to sport and flaunt his presumed, idiosyncratic tastes in dress, food, travel, and the like. The problem for all these multiple sets is not conformity but added novelty.

To add one more paradox, the early theorists of mass society (e.g., Simmel) condemned it because in the vast metropolitan honeycombs people were isolated, transient, anonymous to each other. Americans, sensitive as they are to the criticism of others, took the charge to heart and, in building the postwar suburbs, sought to create fraternity, communality, togetherness, only to find themselves accused of conformity. In the new, recent trend of people returning to the city, it is clear that, in recoil, people will once again establish barriers and will thus bring on the charge, in the next inspection by European sociology, of anonymity, isolation and soullessness, and *anomie*.

One hears the complaint that divorce, crime, and violence demonstrate a widespread social disorganization in the country. But the rising number of divorces may indicate not the disruption of the family but a freer, more individualistic basis of choice and the emergence of the "companionship" marriage. And as regards crime, I have sought to demonstrate . . . that there is actually much *less* crime and violence (though more vicarious violence through movies and TV, and more "windows" onto crime, through the press) than was the case twenty-five and fifty years ago. Certainly Chicago, San Francisco, and New York were much rougher and tougher cities in those years. But violent crime, which is usually a lower-class phenomenon, was then contained within the ecological boundaries of the slum; hence one can recall quiet, tree-lined, crime-free areas and feel that the tenor of life was more even in the past. But a cursory look at the accounts of those days — the descriptions of the gang wars, bordellos, and street-fighting in San Francisco's Barbary Coast, New York's Five Points, or Chicago's First Ward — would show how much more violent the actual life of those cities was in the past.

At this point, it becomes quite apparent that such large-scale abstractions as "the mass society," with the implicit diagnosis of social disorganization and decay that derive from them, are rather meaningless without standards of comparison. Social and cultural change is probably greater and more rapid today in the United States than in any other country, but the assumption that social disorder and *anomie* inevitably attend such change is not borne out in this case.

This may be due to the singular fact that the United States is probably the first large society in history to have change and innovation "built into" its culture. Almost all human societies, traditionalist and habit-ridden as they have been and still are, tend to resist change. The great efforts to industrialize underdeveloped countries, increase worker mobility in Europe, and broaden markets — so necessary to the raising of productivity and standards of living — are again and again frustrated by ingrained resistance to change. Thus, in the Soviet Union, change has been introduced only

by dint of wholesale coercion. In the United States — a culture with no feudal tradition, with a pragmatic ethos, as expressed by Jefferson, that regards God as a "workman"; with a boundless optimism and a restless eagerness for the new that have been bred out of the original conditions of a huge, richly endowed land — change, and the readiness to change, have become the norm. This indeed may be why those consequences of change predicted by theorists basing themselves on European precedent find small confirmation.

The mass society is the product of change — and is itself change. It is the bringing of the "masses" into a society, from which they were once excluded. But the *theory* of the mass society affords us no view of the relations of the parts of the society to each other that would enable us to locate the sources of change. We may not have enough data on which to sketch an alternative theory, but I would argue that certain key factors, in this country at least, deserve to be much more closely examined than they have been: the change from a society once geared to frugal saving and now impelled to spend dizzily; the breakup of family capitalism, with the consequent impact on corporate structure and political power; the centralization of decision-making, politically, in the state and, economically, in a group of large corporate bodies; the rise of status and symbol groups replacing specific interest groups — these indicate that new social forms are in the making and, with them, still greater changes in the complexion of life under mass society. With these may well come new status anxieties — aggravated by the threats of war — changed character structures, and new moral tempers.

The moralist may have his reservations or give approval — as some see in the breakup of the family the loss of a source of essential values, while others see in the new, freer marriages a healthier form of companionship — but the singular fact is that these changes emerge in a society that is now providing one answer to the great challenge posed to Western — and now world — society over the last two hundred years: how, within the frame-work of freedom, to increase the living standards of the majority of people and at the same time maintain or raise cultural levels. For these reasons, the theory of the mass society no longer serves as a description of Western society but as an ideology of romantic protest against contemporary life.

David M. Potter: THE QUEST FOR THE NATIONAL CHARACTER

David Potter is chairman of the Department of History at Stanford. He is a historian who has taken seriously the potential contributions to historical knowledge of the behavioral sciences. He has also tried to preserve the concept of "national character" from the imprecisions to which it has been subjected at the hands of other historians. In this essay he notes the curious individualist-conformist dichotomy in past analyses of the American character around which all these readings have revolved. Potter reviews the debate and then tries to transcend it with an hypothesis of his own.

UNLIKE most nationality groups in the world today, the people of the United States are not ethnically rooted in the land where they live. The French have remote Gallic antecedents; the Germans, Teutonic; the English, Anglo-Saxon; the Italians, Roman; the Irish, Celtic; but the only people in America who can claim ancient American origins are a remnant of Red Indians. In any deep dimension of time, all other Americans are immigrants. They began as Europeans (or in the case of 10 per cent of the population, as Africans), and if they became Americans it was only, somehow, after a relatively recent passage westbound across the Atlantic.

It is, perhaps, this recency of arrival which has given to Americans a some-what compulsive preoccupation with the question of their Americanism. No people can really qualify as a nation in the true sense unless they are united by important qualities or values in common. If they share the same ethnic, or linguistic, or religious, or political heritage, the foundations of nationality can hardly be questioned. But when their ethnic, religious, linguistic, and political heritage is mixed, as in the case of the American people, nationality can hardly exist at all unless it takes the form of a common adjustment to conditions of a new land, a common commitment to shared values, a common esteem for certain qualities of character, or a common set of adaptive traits and attitudes. It is partly for this reason that Americans, although com-

From David M. Potter, "The Quest for National Character," in *The Reconstruction of American History*, John Higham, ed., pp. 197–220. Copyright © Hutchinson and Company Publishers Ltd., 1962. Reprinted by permission of Harper and Row, Publishers, Inc. and of Hutchinson Publishing Group Ltd. For footnotes in full, see the original.

mitted to the principle of freedom of thought, have nevertheless placed such heavy emphasis upon the obligation to accept certain undefined tenets of "Americanism." It is for this same reason, also, that Americans have insisted upon their distinctiveness from the Old World from which they are derived. More than two centuries ago Hector St. John de Crèvecœur asked a famous question, "What then is the American, this new man?" He simply assumed, without arguing the point, that the American is a new man, and he only inquired wherein the American is different. A countless array of writers, including not only careful historians and social scientists but also professional patriots, hit-and-run travellers, itinerant lecturers, intuitive-minded amateurs of all sorts, have been repeating Crèvecœur's question and seeking to answer it ever since.

A thick volume would hardly suffice even to summarize the diverse interpretations which these various writers have advanced in describing or explaining the American character. Almost every trait, good or bad, has been attributed to the American people by someone, and almost every explanation, from Darwinian selection to toilet-training, has been advanced to account for the attributed qualities. But it is probably safe to say that at bottom there have been only two primary ways of explaining the American, and that almost all of the innumerable interpretations which have been formulated can be grouped around or at least oriented to these two basic explanations, which serve as polar points for all the literature.

The most disconcerting fact about these two composite images of the American is that they are strikingly dissimilar and seemingly about as inconsistent with one another as two interpretations of the

same phenomenon could possibly be. One depicts the American primarily as an individualist and an idealist, while the other makes him out as a conformist and a materialist. Both images have been developed with great detail and elaborate explanation in extensive bodies of literature, and both are worth a close scrutiny.

For those who have seen the American primarily as an individualist, the story of his evolution as a distinctive type dates back possibly to the actual moment of his decision to migrate from Europe to the New World, for this was a process in which the daring and venturesome were more prone to risk life in a new country while the timid and the conventional were more disposed to remain at home. If the selective factors in the migration had the effect of screening out men of low initiative, the conditions of life in the North American wilderness, it is argued, must have further heightened the exercise of individual resourcefulness, for they constantly confronted the settler with circumstances in which he could rely upon no one but himself, and where the capacity to improvise a solution for a problem was not infrequently necessary to survival.

In many ways the colonial American exemplified attitudes that were individualistic. Although he made his first settlements by the removal of whole communities which were transplanted bodily — complete with all their ecclesiastical and legal institutions — he turned increasingly, in the later process of settlement, to a more and more individualistic mode of pioneering, in which one separate family would take up title to a separate, perhaps an isolated, tract of land, and would move to this land long in advance of any general settlement, leaving churches and courts and schools far behind. His religion, whether Calvinistic Puritanism or emotional revivalism, made him individually responsible for his own salvation, without the intervention of ecclesiastical intermediaries between himself and his God. His economy, which was based very heavily upon subsistence farming, with very little division of labor, also impelled him to cope with a diversity of problems and to depend upon no one but himself.

With all of these conditions at work, the tendency to place a premium upon individual self-reliance was no doubt well developed long before the cult of the American as an individualist crystallized in a conceptual form. But it did crystallize, and it took on almost its classic formulation in the thought of Thomas Jefferson.

It may seem paradoxical to regard Jefferson as a delineator of American national character, for in direct terms he did not attempt to describe the American character at all. But he did conceive that one particular kind of society was necessary to the fulfillment of American ideals, and further that one particular kind of person, namely the independent farmer, was a necessary component in the optimum society. He believed that the principles of liberty and equality, which he cherished so deeply, could not exist in a hierarchical society, such as that of Europe, nor, indeed, in any society where economic and social circumstances enabled one set of men to dominate and exploit the rest. An urban society or a commercial society, with its concentration of financial power into a few hands and its imposition of dependence through a wage system, scarcely lent itself better than an aristocracy to his basic values. In fact, only a society of small husbandmen who tilled their own soil and found sustenance in their own produce could

achieve the combination of independence and equalitarianism which he envisioned for the ideal society. Thus, although Jefferson did not write a description of the national character, he erected a model for it, and the model ultimately had more influence than a description could ever have exercised. The model American was a plain, straightforward agrarian democrat, an individualist in his desire for freedom for himself, and an idealist in his desire for equality for all men.

Jefferson's image of the American as a man of independence, both in his values and in his mode of life, has had immense appeal to Americans ever since. They found this image best exemplified in the man of the frontier, for he, as a pioneer, seemed to illustrate the qualities of independence and self-reliance in their most pronounced and most dramatic form. Thus in a tradition of something like folklore, half-legendary figures like Davy Crockett have symbolized America as well as symbolizing the frontier. In literature, ever since J. Fenimore Cooper's Leatherstocking tales, the frontier scout, at home under the open sky, free from the trammels of an organized and stratified society, has been cherished as an incarnation of American qualities. In American politics the voters showed such a marked preference for men who had been born in log cabins that many an ambitious candidate pretended to pioneer origins which were in fact fictitious.

The pioneer is, of course, not necessarily an agrarian (he may be a hunter, a trapper, a cowboy, a prospector for gold), and the agrarian is not necessarily a pioneer (he may be a European peasant tilling his ancestral acres), but the American frontier was basically an agricultural frontier, and the pioneer was usually a farmer. Thus it was possible to make an equation between the pioneer and the agrarian, and since the pioneer evinced the agrarian traits in their most picturesque and most appealing form there was a strong psychological impulse to concentrate the diffused agrarian ideal into a sharp frontier focus. This is, in part, what Frederick Jackson Turner did in 1893 when he wrote *The Significance of the Frontier in American History*. In this famous essay Turner offered an explanation of what has been distinctive in American history, but it is not as widely realized as it might be that he also penned a major contribution to the literature of national character. Thus Turner affirmed categorically that "The American intellect owes its striking characteristics to the frontier. That coarseness and strength, combined with acuteness and acquisitiveness; that practical inventive turn of mind, quick to find expedients; that masterful grasp of material things, lacking in the artistic but powerful to effect great ends; that restless, nervous energy; that dominant individualism, working for good and for evil; and withal, that buoyancy and exuberance which comes with freedom — these are traits of the frontier, or traits called out elsewhere because of the existence of the frontier."

A significant but somewhat unnoticed aspect of Turner's treatment is the fact that, in his quest to discover the traits of the American character, he relied for proof not upon descriptive evidence that given traits actually prevailed, but upon the argument that given conditions in the environment would necessarily cause the development of certain traits. Thus the cheapness of land on the frontier would make for universal land-holding which in turn would make for equalitarianism in the society. The absence of division of labor on the frontier would force each man to do most things for himself, and

this would breed self-reliance. The pitting of the individual man against the elemental forces of the wilderness and of nature would further reinforce this self-reliance. Similarly, the fact that a man had moved out in advance of society's institutions and its stratified structure would mean that he could find independence, without being overshadowed by the institutions, and could enjoy an equality unknown to stratified society. All of this argument was made without any sustained effort to measure exactly how much recognizable equalitarianism and individualism and self-reliance actually were in evidence either on the American frontier or in American society. There is little reason to doubt that most of his arguments were valid or that most of the traits which he emphasized did acually prevail, but it is nevertheless ironical that Turner's interpretation, which exercised such vast influence upon historians, was not based upon the historian's kind of proof, which is from evidence, but upon an argument from logic which so often fails to work out in historical experience.

But no matter how he arrived at it, Turner's picture reaffirmed some by-now-familiar beliefs about the American character. The American was equalitarian, stoutly maintaining the practices of both social and political democracy; he had a spirit of freedom reflected in his buoyance and exuberance; he was individualistic — hence "practical and inventive," "quick to find expedients," "restless, nervous, acquisitive." Turner was too much a scholar to let his evident fondness for the frontiersman run away with him entirely, and he took pains to point out that this development was not without its sordid aspects. There was a marked primitivism about the frontier, and with it, to some extent, a regression from civilized standards. The buoyant and exuberant frontiersman sometimes emulated his Indian neighbors in taking the scalps of his adversaries. Coarse qualities sometimes proved to have more survival value than gentle ones. But on the whole this regression was brief, and certainly a rough-and-ready society had its compensating advantages. Turner admired his frontiersman, and thus Turner's American, like Jefferson's American, was partly a realistic portrait from life and partly an idealized model from social philosophy. Also, though one of these figures was an agrarian and the other was a frontiersman, both were very much the same man — democratic, freedom-loving, self-reliant, and individualistic.

An essay like this is hardly the place to prove either the validity or the invalidity of the Jeffersonian and Turnerian conception of the American character. The attempt to do so would involve a review of the entire range of American historical experience, and in the course of such a review the proponents of this conception could point to a vast body of evidence in support of their interpretation. They could argue, with much force, that Americans have consistently been zealous to defend individualism by defending the rights and the welfare of the individual, and that our whole history is a protracted record of our government's recognizing its responsibility to an ever broader range of people — to men without property, to men held in slavery, to women, to small enterprises threatened by monopoly, to children laboring in factories, to industrial workers, to the ill, to the elderly, and to the unemployed. This record, it can further be argued, is also a record of the practical idealism of the American people, unceasingly at work.

But without attempting a verdict on the historical validity of this image of the American as individualist and idealist, it is important to bear in mind that this image has been partly a portrait, but also partly a model. In so far as it is a portrait — a likeness by an observer reporting on Americans whom he knew — it can be regarded as authentic testimony on the American character. But in so far as it is a model — an idealization of what is best in Americanism, and of what Americans should strive to be, it will only be misleading if used as evidence of what ordinary Americans are like in their everyday lives. It is also important to recognize that the Jefferson-Turner image posited several traits as distinctively American, and that they are not all necessarily of equal validity. Particularly, Jefferson and Turner both believed that love of equality and love of liberty go together. For Jefferson the very fact, stated in the Declaration of Independence, that "all men are created equal," carried with it the corollary that they are all therefore "entitled to [and would be eager for] life, liberty, and the pursuit of happiness." From this premise it is easy to slide imperceptibly into the position of holding that equalitarianism and individualism are inseparably linked, or even that they are somehow the same thing. This is, indeed, almost an officially sanctioned ambiguity in the American creed. But it requires only a little thoughtful reflection to recognize that equalitarianism and individualism do not necessarily go together. Alexis de Tocqueville understood this fact more than a century ago, and out of his recognition he framed an analysis which is not only the most brilliant single account of the American character, but is also the only major alternative to the Jefferson-Turner image.

After travelling the length and breadth of the United States for ten months at the height of Andrew Jackson's ascendancy,

Tocqueville felt no doubt of the depth of the commitment of Americans to democracy. Throughout two volumes which ranged over every aspect of American life, he consistently emphasized democracy as a pervasive factor. But the democracy which he wrote about was far removed from Thomas Jefferson's dream. "Liberty," he observed of the Americans, "is not the chief object of their desires; equality is their idol. They make rapid and sudden efforts to obtain liberty, and if they miss their aim resign themselves to their disappointment; but nothing can satisfy them without equality, and they would rather perish than lose it."

This emphasis upon equality was not, in itself, inconsistent with the most orthodox Jeffersonian ideas, and indeed Tocqueville took care to recognize that under certain circumstances equality and freedom might "meet and blend." But such circumstances would be rare, and the usual effects of equality would be to encourage conformity and discourage individualism, to regiment opinion and to inhibit dissent. Tocqueville justified this seeming paradoxical conclusion by arguing that:

When the inhabitant of a democratic country compares himself individually with all those about him, he feels with pride that he is the equal of any one of them; but when he comes to survey the totality of his fellows, and to place himself in contrast with so huge a body, he is instantly overwhelmed by the sense of his own insignificance and weakness. The same equality that renders him independent of each of his fellow citizens, taken severally, exposes him alone and unprotected to the influence of the greater number. The public, therefore, among a democratic people, has a singular power, which aristocratic nations cannot conceive; for it does not persuade others to its beliefs, but it imposes them and makes them permeate the thinking of everyone by a sort of enormous pressure of the mind of all upon the individual intelligence.

At the time when Tocqueville wrote, he expressed admiration for the American people in many ways, and when he criticized adversely his tone was abstract, bland, and free of the petulance and the personalities that characterized some critics, like Mrs. Trollope and Charles Dickens. Consequently, Tocqueville was relatively well received in the United States, and we have largely forgotten what a severe verdict his observations implied. But, in fact, he pictured the American character as the very embodiment of conformity, of conformity so extreme that not only individualism but even freedom was endangered. Because of the enormous weight with which the opinion of the majority pressed upon the individual, Tocqueville said, the person in the minority "not only mistrusts his strength, but even doubts of his right; and he is very near acknowledging that he is in the wrong when the greater number of his countrymen assert that he is so. The majority do not need to force him; they convince him." "The principle of equality," as a consequence, had the effect of "prohibiting him from thinking at all," and "freedom of opinion does not exist in America." Instead of reinforcing liberty, therefore, equality constituted a danger to liberty. It caused the majority "to despise and undervalue the rights of private persons," and led on to the pessimistic conclusion that "Despotism appears . . . peculiarly to be dreaded in democratic times."

Tocqueville was perhaps the originator of the criticism of the American as conformist, but he also voiced another criticism which has had many echoes, but which did not originate with him. This was the condemnation of the American as a materialist. As early as 1805 Richard Parkinson had observed that "all men there [in America] make it [money] their pursuit," and in 1823 William Faux had asserted that "two selfish gods, pleasure and gain, enslave the Americans." In the interval between the publication of the first and second parts of Tocqueville's study, Washington Irving coined his classic phrase concerning "the almighty dollar, that great object of universal devotion throughout the land." But it remained for Tocqueville, himself, to link materialism with equality, as he had already linked conformity.

Of all passions [he said] which originate in or are fostered by equality, there is one which it renders peculiarly intense, and which it also infuses into the heart of every man: I mean the love of well-being. The taste for well-being is the prominent and indelible feature of democratic times. . . . The effort to satisfy even the least wants of the body and to provide the little conveniences of life is uppermost in every mind.

He described this craving for physical comforts as a "passion," and affirmed that "I know of no country, indeed, where the love of money has taken stronger hold on the affections of men."

For more than a century we have lived with the contrasting images of the American character which Thomas Jefferson and Alexis de Tocqueville visualized. Both of these images presented the American as an equalitarian and therefore as a democrat, but one was an agrarian democrat while the other was a majoritarian democrat; one an independent individualist, the other a mass-dominated conformist; one an idealist, the other a materialist. Through many decades of self-scrutiny Americans have been seeing one or the other of these images whenever they looked into the mirror of self-analysis.

The discrepancy between the two images is so great that it must bring the searcher for the American character up with a jerk, and must force him to grapple with the question whether these seemingly antithetical versions of the American can be reconciled in any way. Can the old familiar formula for embracing opposite reports — that the situation presents a paradox — be stretched to encompass both Tocqueville and Jefferson? Or is there so grave a flaw somewhere that one must question the whole idea of national character and call to mind all the warnings that thoughtful men have uttered against the very concept that national groups can be distinguished from one another in terms of collective group traits.

Certainly there is a sound enough basis for doubting the validity of generalizations about national character. To begin with, many of these generalizations have been derived not from any dispassionate observation or any quest for truth, but from superheated patriotism which sought only to glorify one national group by invidious comparison with other national groups, or from a pseudoscientific racism which claimed innately superior qualities for favored ethnic groups. Further, the explanations which were offered to account for the ascribed traits were as suspect as the ascriptions themselves. No one today will accept the notions which once prevailed that such qualities as the capacity for self-government are inherited in the genes, nor will anyone credit the notion that national character is a unique quality which manifests itself mystically in all the inhabitants of a given country. Between the chauvinistic purposes for which the concept of national character was used, and the irrationality with which it was supported, it fell during the 1930's into a disrepute from which it has by no means fully recovered.

Some thinkers of a skeptical turn of mind had rejected the idea of national character even at a time when most historians accepted it without question. Thus, for instance, John Stuart Mill as early as 1849 observed that "of all vulgar modes of escaping from the consideration of the effect of social and moral influences on the human mind, the most vulgar is that of attributing diversities of character to inherent natural differences." Sir John Seeley said, "no explanation is so vague, so cheap, and so difficult to verify."

But it was particularly at the time of the rise of Fascism and Naziism, when the vicious aspects of extreme nationalism and of racism became glaringly conspicuous, that historians in general began to repudiate the idea of national character and to disavow it as an intellectual concept, even though they sometimes continued to employ it as a working device in their treatment of the peoples with whose history they were concerned. To historians whose skepticism had been aroused, the conflicting nature of the images of the American as an individualistic democrat or as a conformist democrat would have seemed simply to illustrate further the already demonstrated flimsiness and fallacious quality of all generalizations about national character.

But to deny that the inhabitants of one country may, as a group, evince a given trait in higher degree than the inhabitants of some other country amounts almost to a denial that the culture of one people can be different from the culture of another people. To escape the pitfalls of racism in this way is to fly from one error into the embrace of another, and students of culture — primarily anthro-pologists, rather than historians — perceived that rejection of the idea that a group could be distinctive, along with the idea that the distinction was eternal and immutable in the genes, involved the ancient logical fallacy of throwing out the baby along with the bath. Accordingly, the study of national character came under the special sponsorship of cultural anthropology, and in the 'forties a number of outstanding workers in this field tackled the problem of national character, including the American character, with a methodological precision and objectivity that had never been applied to the subject before. After their investigations, they felt no doubt that national character was a reality — an observable and demonstrable reality. One of them, Margaret Mead, declared that "In every culture, in Samoa, in Germany, in Iceland, in Bali, and in the United States of America, we will find consistencies and regularities in the way in which new born babies grow up and assume the attitudes and behavior patterns of their elders — and this we may call 'character formation.' We will find that Samoans may be said to have a Samoan character structure and Americans an American character structure." Another, the late Clyde Kluckhohn, wrote: "The statistical prediction can safely be made that a hundred Americans, for example, will display certain defined characteristics more frequently than will a hundred Englishmen comparably distributed as to age, sex, social class, and vocations."

If these new students were correct, it meant that there was some kind of identifiable American character. It might conform to the Jeffersonian image; it might conform to the Tocquevillian image; it might conform in part to both; or it might conform to neither. But in any event discouraged investigators were enjoined against giving up the quest with the conclusion that there is no American character. It has been said that a philosopher is a blind man in a dark room looking for a black cat that isn't there; the student of national character might also, at times, resemble a blind man in a dark room, looking for a black cat, but the cultural anthropologists exhorted him to persevere in spite of the problems of visibility, for the cat was indubitably there.

Still confronted with the conflicting images of the agrarian democrat and the majoritarian democrat, the investigator might avoid an outright rejection of either by taking the position that the American character has changed, and that each of these images was at one time valid and realistic, but that in the twentieth century the qualities of conformity and materialism have grown increasingly prominent, while the qualities of individualism and idealism have diminished. This interpretation of a changing American character has had a number of adherents in the last two decades, for it accords well with the observation that the conditions of the American culture have changed. As they do so, of course the qualities of a character that is derived from the culture might be expected to change correspondingly. Thus, Henry S. Commager, in his *The American Mind* (1950), portrayed in two contrasting chapters "the nineteenth-century American" and "the twentieth-century American." Similarly, David Riesman, in *The Lonely Crowd* (1950), significantly sub-titled *A Study of the Changing American Character*, pictured two types of Americans, first an "inner-directed man," whose values were deeply internalized and who adhered to these values tenaciously, regardless of the opinions of his peers (clearly an individualist), and second an "other-directed man," who sub-

ordinated his own internal values to the changing expectations directed toward him by changing peer groups (in short, a conformist).

Although he viewed his inner-directed man as having been superseded historically by his other-directed man, Riesman did not attempt to explain in historical terms the reason for the change. He made a rather limited effort to relate his stages of character formation to stages of population growth, but he has since then not used population phase as a key. Meanwhile, it is fairly clear, from Riesman's own context, as well as from history in general, that there were changes in the culture which would have accounted for the transition in character. Most nineteenth-century Americans were self-employed; most were engaged in agriculture; most produced a part of their own food and clothing. These facts meant that their well-being did not depend on the goodwill or the services of their associates, but upon their resourcefulness in wrestling with the elemental forces of Nature. Even their physical isolation from their fellows added something to the independence of their natures. But most twentieth-century Americans work for wages or salaries, many of them in very large employee groups; most are engaged in office or factory work; most are highly specialized, and are reliant upon many others to supply their needs in an economy with an advanced division of labor. Men now do depend upon the goodwill and the services of their fellows. This means that what they achieve depends less upon stamina and hardihood than upon their capacity to get along with other people and to fit smoothly into a co-operative relationship. In short the culture now places a premium upon the qualities which will enable the individual to function effectively as a member of a large organizational group. The strategic importance of this institutional factor has been well recognized by William H. Whyte, Jr., in his significantly titled book *The Organization Man* (1956) — for the conformity of Whyte's bureaucratized individual results from the fact that he lives under an imperative to succeed in a situation where promotion and even survival depend upon effective inter-action with others in an hierarchical structure.

Thus, by an argument from logic (always a treacherous substitute for direct observation in historical study), one can make a strong case that the nineteenth-century American should have been (and therefore must have been) an individualist, while the twentieth-century American should be (and therefore is) a conformist. But this formula crashes headlong into the obdurate fact that no Americans have ever been more classically conformist than Tocqueville's Jacksonian democrats — hardy specimens of the frontier breed, far back in the nineteenth century, long before the age of corporate images, peer groups, marginal differentiation, and status frustration. In short, Tocqueville's nineteenth-century American, whether frontiersman or no, was to some extent an other-directed man. Carl N. Degler has pointed out this identity in a very cogent paper not yet published, in which he demonstrates very forcibly that most of our easy assumptions about the immense contrast between the nineteenth-century American and the twentieth-century American are vulnerable indeed.

This conclusion should, perhaps, have been evident from the outset, in view of the fact that it was Tocqueville who, in the nineteenth century, gave us the image which we now frequently identify as the twentieth-century American. But in any case, the fact that he did so means that we can hardly resolve the dilemma of our individualist democrat and our majoritarian democrat by assuming that both are historically valid but that one replaced the other. The problem of determining what use we can make of either of these images, in view of the fact that each casts doubt upon the other, still remains. Is it possible to uncover common factors in these apparently contradictory images, and thus to make use of them both in our quest for a definition of the national character? For no matter whether either of these versions of the American is realistic as a type or image, there is no doubt that both of them reflect fundamental aspects of the American experience.

There is no purpose, at this point in this essay, to execute a neat, pre-arranged sleight-of-hand by which the individualist democrat and the conformist democrat will cast off their disguises and will reveal themselves as identical twin Yankee Doodle Dandies, both born on the fourth of July. On the contrary, intractable, irresolvable discrepancies exist between the two figures, and it will probably never be possible to go very far in the direction of accepting the one without treating the other as a fictitious image, to be rejected as reflecting an anti-democratic bias and as at odds with the evidence from actual observation of the behavior of *Homo americanus* in his native haunts. At the same time, however, it is both necessary to probe for the common factors, and legitimate to observe that there is one common factor conspicuous in the extreme — namely the emphasis on equality, so dear both to Jefferson's American and to Tocqueville's. One of these figures, it will be recalled, has held no truth to be more self-evident than that all men are created equal, while the other has made equality his "idol," far more jealously guarded than his liberty.

If the commitment to equality is so dominant a feature in both of these representations of the American, it will perhaps serve as a key to various facets of the national character, even to contradictory aspects of this character. In a society as complex as that of the United States, in fact, it may be that the common factors underlying the various manifestations are all that our quest should seek. For it is evident that American life and American energy have expressed themselves in a great diversity of ways, and any effort to define the American as if nearly two hundred million persons all corresponded to a single type would certainly reduce complex data to a blunt, crude, and oversimplified form. To detect what qualities Americans share in their diversity may be far more revealing than to superimpose the stereotype of a fictitious uniformity. If this is true, it means that our quest must be to discover the varied and dissimilar ways in which the commitment to equality expresses itself — the different forms which it takes in different individuals — rather than to regard it as an undifferentiated component which shows in all individuals in the same way. Figuratively, one might say that in seeking for what is common, one should think of the metal from which Americans are forged, no matter into how many shapes this metal may be cast, rather than thinking of a die with which they all are stamped into an identical shape. If the problem is viewed in this way, it will be readily apparent that Tocqueville made a pregnant statement when he observed that the idea of equality was "the funda-mental fact from which all others seem to be derived."

The term "equality" is a loose-fitting garment and it has meant very different things at very different times. It is very frequently used to imply parity or uniformity. The grenadiers in the King of Prussia's guard were equal in that they were all, uniformly, over six feet six inches tall. Particularly, it can mean, and often does mean in some social philosophies, uniformity of material welfare — of income, of medical care, etc. But people are clearly not uniform in strength or intelligence or beauty, and one must ask, therefore, what kind of uniformity Americans believed in. Did they believe in an equal sharing of goods? Tocqueville himself answered this question when he said, "I know of no country . . . where a profounder contempt is expressed for the theory of the permanent equality of property."

At this point in the discussion of equality, someone, and very likely a business man, is always likely to break in with the proposition that Americans believe in equality of opportunity — in giving everyone what is called an equal start, and in removing all handicaps such as illiteracy and all privileges such as monopoly or special priority, which will tend to give one person an advantage over another. But if a person gains the advantage without having society give it to him, by being more clever or more enterprising or even just by being stronger than someone else, he is entitled to enjoy the benefits that accrue from these qualities, particularly in terms of possessing more property or wealth than others.

Historically, equality of opportunity was a particularly apt form of equalitarianism for a new, undeveloped frontier country. In the early stages of American history, the developed resources of the country were so few that an equality in the division of these assets would only have meant an insufficiency for everyone. The best economic benefit which the government could give was to offer a person free access in developing undeveloped resources for his own profit, and this is what America did offer. It was an ideal formula for everyone: for the individual it meant a very real chance to gain more wealth than he would have secured by receiving an equal share of the existing wealth. For the community, it meant that no one could prosper appreciably without activities which would develop undeveloped resources, at a time when society desperately needed rapid economic development. For these reasons, equality of opportunity did become the most highly sanctioned form of equalitarianism in the United States.

Because of this sanction, Americans have indeed been tolerant of great discrepancies in wealth. They have approved of wealth much more readily when they believed that it had been earned — as in the case, for instance, of Henry Ford — than when they thought it had been acquired by some special privilege or monopoly. In general, however, they have not merely condoned great wealth; they have admired it. But to say that the ideal of equality means only equality of opportunity is hardly to tell the whole story. The American faith has also held, with intense conviction, the belief that all men are equal in the sense that they share a common humanity — that all are alike in the eyes of God — and that every person has a certain dignity, no matter how low his circumstances, which no one else, no matter how high *his* circumstances, is entitled to disregard. When this concept of the nature of man

was translated into a system of social arrangements, the crucial point on which it came to focus was the question of rank. For the concept of rank essentially denies that all men are equally worthy and argues that some are better than others — that some are born to serve and others born to command. The American creed not only denied this view, but even condemned it and placed a taboo upon it. Some people, according to the American creed, might be more fortunate than others, but they must never regard themselves as better than others. Pulling one's rank has therefore been the unforgivable sin against American democracy, and the American people have, accordingly, reserved their heartiest dislike for the officer class in the military, for people with upstage or condescending manners, and for anyone who tries to convert power or wealth (which are not resented) into overt rank or privilege (which are). Thus it is permissible for an American to have servants (which is a matter of function), but he must not put them in livery (which is a matter of rank); permissible to attend expensive schools, but not to speak with a cultivated accent; permissible to rise in the world, but never to repudiate the origins from which he rose. The most palpable and overt possible claim of rank is, of course, the effort of one individual to assert authority, in a personal sense, over others, and accordingly the rejection of authority is the most pronounced of all the concrete expressions of American beliefs in equality.

In almost any enterprise which involves numbers of people working in conjunction, it is necessary for some people to tell other people what to do. This function cannot be wholly abdicated without causing a breakdown, and in America it cannot be exercised overtly without violating the taboos against authority. The result is that the American people have developed an arrangement which skillfully combines truth and fiction, and maintains that the top man does not rule, but leads; and does not give orders, but calls signals; while the men in the lower echelons are not underlings, but members of the team. This view of the relationship is truthful in the sense that the man in charge does depend upon his capacity to elicit the voluntary or spontaneous co-operation of the members of his organization, and he regards the naked use of authority to secure compliance as an evidence of failure; also, in many organizations, the members lend their support willingly, and contribute much more on a voluntary basis than authority could ever exact from them. But the element of fiction sometimes enters, in terms of the fact that both sides understand that in many situations authority would have to be invoked if voluntary compliance were not forthcoming. This would be humiliating to all parties — to the top man because it would expose his failure as a leader and to the others because it would force them to recognize the carefully concealed fact that in an ultimate sense they are subject to coercion. To avoid this mutually undesirable exploration of the ultimate implications, both sides recognize that even when an order has to be given, it is better for it to be expressed in the form of a request or a proposal, and when compliance is mandatory, it should be rendered with an appearance of consent.

It is in this way that the anti-authoritarian aspect of the creed of equality leads to the extraordinarily strong emphasis upon permissiveness, either as a reality or as a mere convention in American life. So strong is the taboo against authority that the father, once a paternal authority, is now expected to be a pal to his children, and to persuade rather than to command. The husband, once a lord and master, to be obeyed under the vows of matrimony, is now a partner. And if, perchance, an adult male in command of the family income uses his control to bully his wife and children, he does not avow his desire to make them obey, but insists that he only wants them to be co-operative. The unlimited American faith in the efficacy of discussion as a means of finding solutions for controversies reflects less a faith in the powers of rational persuasion than a supreme reluctance to let anything reach a point where authority will have to be invoked. If hypocrisy is the tribute that vice pays to virtue, permissiveness is, to some extent, the tribute that authority pays to the principle of equality.

When one recognizes some of these varied strands in the fabric of equalitarianism it becomes easier to see how the concept has contributed to the making, both of the Jeffersonian American and the Tocquevillian American. For as one picks at the strands they ravel out in quite dissimilar directions. The strand of equality of opportunity, for instance, if followed out, leads to the theme of individualism. It challenged each individual to pit his skill and talents in a competition against the skill and talents of others and to earn the individual rewards which talent and effort might bring. Even more, the imperatives of the competitive race were so compelling that the belief grew up that everyone had a kind of obligation to enter his talents in this competition and to "succeed." It was but a step from the belief that ability and virtue would produce success to the belief that success was produced by — and was therefore an evidence of — ability and virtue. In short, money not only represented power, it also was a sign of the presence of admirable qualities in the man who attained it. Here, certainly, an equalitarian doctrine fostered materialism, and if aggressiveness and competitiveness are individualistic qualities, then it fostered individualism also.

Of course, neither American individualism nor American materialism can be explained entirely in these terms. Individualism must have derived great strength, for instance, from the reflection that if all men are equal, a man might as well form his own convictions as accept the convictions of someone else no better than himself. It must also have been reinforced by the frontier experience, which certainly compelled every man to rely upon himself. But this kind of individualism is not the quality of independent-mindedness, and it is not the quality which Tocqueville was denying when he said that Americans were conformists. A great deal of confusion has resulted, in the discussion of the American character, from the fact that the term individualism is sometimes used (as by Tocqueville) to mean willingness to think and act separately from the majority, and sometimes (as by Turner) to mean capacity to get along without help. It might be supposed that the two would converge, on the theory that a man who can get along by himself without help will soon recognize that he may as well also think for himself without help. But in actuality, this did not necessarily happen. Self-reliance on the frontier was more a matter of courage and of staying power than of intellectual resourcefulness, for the struggle with the wilderness challenged the body rather than the mind, and a man might be supremely effective in fending for himself, and at the same time

supremely conventional in his ideas. In this sense, Turner's individualist is not really an antithesis of Tocqueville's conformist at all.

Still, it remains true that Jefferson's idealist and Tocqueville's conformist both require explanation, and that neither can be accounted for in the terms which make Jefferson's individualist and Tocqueville's materialist understandable. As an explanation of these facets of the American character, it would seem that the strand of equalitarianism which stresses the universal dignity of all men, and which hates rank as a violation of dignity, might be found quite pertinent. For it is the concept of the worth of every man which has stimulated a century and a half of reform, designed at every step to realize in practice the ideal that every human possesses potentialities which he should have a chance to fulfill. Whatever has impeded this fulfillment, whether it be lack of education, chattel slavery, the exploitation of the labor of unorganized workers, the hazards of unemployment, or the handicaps of age and infirmity, has been the object, at one time or another, of a major reforming crusade. The whole American commitment to progress would be impossible without a prior belief in the perfectibility of man and in the practicability of steps to bring perfection nearer. In this sense, the American character has been idealistic. And yet its idealism is not entirely irreconcilable with its materialism, for American idealism has often framed its most altruistic goals in materialistic terms — for instance of raising the standard of living as a means to a better life. Moreover, Americans are committed to the view that materialistic means are necessary to idealistic ends. Franklin defined what is necessary to a virtuous life by saying "an empty sack cannot stand upright," and

Americans have believed that spiritual and humanitarian goals are best achieved by instrumentalities such as universities and hospitals which carry expensive price tags.

If the belief that all men are of equal worth has contributed to a feature of American life so much cherished as our tradition of humanitarian reform, how could it at the same time have contributed to a feature so much deplored as American conformity? Yet it has done both, for the same respect of the American for his fellow men, which has made many a reformer think that his fellow citizens are worth helping, has also made many another American think that he has no business to question the opinions that his neighbors have sanctioned. True, he says, if all men are equal, each ought to think for himself, but on the other hand, no man should consider himself better than his neighbors, and if the majority have adopted an opinion on a matter, how can one man question their opinion, without setting himself up as being better than they. Moreover, it is understood that the majority are pledged not to force him to adopt their opinion. But it is also understood that in return for this immunity he will voluntarily accept the will of the majority in most things. The absence of a formal compulsion to conform seemingly increases the obligation to conform voluntarily. Thus, the other-directed man is seen to be derived as much from the American tradition of equalitarianism as the rugged individualist, and the compulsive seeker of an unequally large share of wealth as much as the humanitarian reformer striving for the fulfillment of democratic ideals.

To say that they are all derived from the same tradition is by no means to say that they are, in some larger, mystic sense, all the same. They are not, even though the idealism of the reformer may seek materialistic goals, and though men who are individualists in their physical lives may be conformists in their ideas. But all of them, it may be argued, do reflect circumstances which are distinctively American, and all present manifestations of a character which is more convincingly American because of its diversity than any wholly uniform character could possibly be. If Americans have never reached the end of their quest for an image that would represent the American character, it may be not because they failed to find one image but because they failed to recognize the futility of attempting to settle upon one, and the necessity of accepting several.

Francis L. K. Hsu: TWO WAYS OF LIFE

If foreign observers of America possess an advantage over the native in seeing the subject from a comparative perspective, then it follows that comparison of the United States with other than European cultures may have a special value. An arresting angle of vision is offered by anthropologist Francis L. K. Hsu of Northwestern University in Americans and Chinese, *one of the regrettably few studies which systematically compare two contemporary national cultures. Hsu, an American citizen who terms himself a "marginal man," was born and raised in China, where he lived until the outbreak of the Second World War.*

THE CHINESE and American ways of life may be reduced to two sets of contrasts. First, in the American way of life the emphasis is placed upon the predilections of the individual, a characteristic we shall call *individual-centered*. This is in contrast to the emphasis the Chinese put upon an individual's appropriate place and behavior among his fellowmen, a characteristic we shall term *situation-centered*. The second fundamental contrast is the prominence of emotions in the American way of life as compared with the tendency of the Chinese to underplay all matters of the heart.

These two sets of contrasts are interrelated. Being individual-centered, the American moves toward social and psychological isolation. His happiness tends to be unqualified ecstasy just as his sorrow is likely to mean unbearable misery. A strong emotionality is inevitable because the emotions are concentrated in one individual.

Being more situation-centered, the Chinese is inclined to be socially or psychologically dependent on others, for this situation-centered individual is tied closer to his world and his fellowmen. His happiness and his sorrow tend to be mild because they are shared.

These contrasting ways of life — the individual-centered American way and the situation-centered Chinese way — will, then, be our key to all the chapters which follow. This key, I believe, will open a new door to understanding the two peoples' differences in social life, government, religion and economy. We shall find also that this fundamental contrast is at the core of the unique and

deeply embedded problems and weaknesses which plague each society, such as racial intolerance in America and the lack of science in China. . . .

THE HOME

Let us begin with Chinese and American homes. An American house usually has a yard, large or small. It may have a hedge, but rarely is there a wall so high that a passer-by cannot see the windows. The majority of American houses have neither hedge nor wall whatsoever. Usually the interior is shielded from exterior view only by window curtains or blinds, and then during but part of the day.

The majority of Chinese houses are, in the first place, surrounded by such high walls that only the roofs are visible from the outside, and solid gates separate the interior grounds from the outside world. In addition there is usually a shadow wall placed directly in front of the gates on the other side of the street as well as a four-leafed wooden screen standing about five feet behind the gates. The outside shadow wall keeps the home from direct exposure to the unseen spirits. The inside wooden screen shields the interior courtyard from pedestrians' glances when the gates are ajar.

Inside the home, the contrast between China and America is reversed. The American emphasis within the home is on privacy. There are not only doors to the bathrooms but also to the bedrooms, to the living room, and even to the kitchen. Space and possessions are individualized. Thus parents have little liberty in the rooms of the children, and children cannot do what they want in those parts of the house regarded as pre-eminently the domain of the parents. Among some sections of the American population this rule of privacy extends to the husband and wife, so that each has a separate bedroom.

Within the Chinese home, on the other hand, privacy hardly exists at all, except between opposite sexes who are not spouses. Chinese children, even in the homes which have ample room, tend to share the same chambers with their parents until they reach adolescence. Not only do parents have freedom of action with reference to the children's belongings, but the youngsters can also use the possessions of the parents if they can lay their hands on them. If children damage their parents' possessions they are scolded not because they touched things that were not theirs but because they are too young to handle them with proper care.

The lack of privacy within the home finds its extreme expression in many well-to-do families of North China. Here the rooms are arranged in rows like the cars of a train. But instead of each room having a separate entrance, all the rooms are arranged in sequence, one leading into another. Thus, if there are five rooms, the front door of the house opens into the center room, which serves as the kitchen and dining room. There are two doors on opposite walls of the kitchen, each leading into a room which has in turn another door opening into the end rooms. Beginning at one end of the house, call it room A, one can walk in a straight line from there to room B, into the kitchen-dining room C, into room D, and finally into room E. The parents will occupy room B, nearest the kitchen, leaving room A free for a married daughter when she and her children come for a prolonged visit. If the family has two married sons, the older brother and his wife and children will occupy room D, while the younger brother and his wife will occupy room E. The occupants of rooms A and E will have to cross, respectively, rooms B and D in order to go in and out of the house. Actual arrangements vary somewhat from family to family, but this simplified picture is generally true.

Such an arrangement in living quarters would be very offensive to Americans. For even within the family Americans hew to the line as to what is yours and what is mine. But many Chinese adhere to a variation of the common linear arrangement even when they have more rooms in which to spread out. For they consider all within the four walls as being one body. The American child's physical environment establishes strong lines of individual distinction within the home but there is very little stress on separation of the home from the community. The Chinese child's environment is exactly the reverse. He finds a home with few demarcation lines within it but separated by high walls and multiple gates from the outside world.

PARENTS AND CHILDREN

The difference between Chinese and American homes reflects their contrasting patterns of behavior in the family. In no country on earth is there so much attention paid to infancy and so much privilege accorded childhood as in the United States. From every point of view this country is a paradise on earth for children. In contrast, it may be said without exaggeration that China is a country in which children come last.

The contrast can be seen in a myriad of ways. Americans are very verbal about their children's rights. There is not only state and federal legislation to protect the young ones, but there are also various juvenile protective associations to look after their welfare. Not only is infanticide treated like murder, but parents can get into legal trouble if they discipline their children with some enthusiasm.

In China parents have a completely free hand with their children. Popular misconception notwithstanding, infanticide has always been rare in China, and certainly no parents would brag about it. Yet even in modern times parents who have committed infanticide have almost always been free from legal action. It is literally true that from the viewpoint of American children, parents have practically no rights; but from the viewpoint of Chinese parents, children have little reason to expect protection from their elders. If an American were to point with justifiable pride to his country's many child protective associations, a Chinese would simply counter with an equally proud boast about his nation's numerous "societies for saving papers with written characters on" or "societies for giving away coffins."

American parents are so concerned with the welfare of their children, and they are so determined to do the right thing, that they handsomely support a huge number of child specialists, scientific or quack, to supply them with advice on what children like best. Chinese parents have taken their children so much for granted that pediatrics as a separate branch of medicine was unknown until modern times. As far as I know there is no piece of traditional literature aimed at making the Chinese better parents, and even during the days of the Republic there was hardly any scientific inquiry into what the children might think and desire. Articles on how to treat children appeared only sporadically in a few Chinese newspapers and magazines.

But Americans do not only study their children's behavior — they glorify it. Chinese do not only take their children for granted — they minimize them. The important thing to Americans is what parents should do for their children; to Chinese, what children should do for their parents.

The American emphasis on children has gone so far that even strangers can interfere with parents without regard to the circumstances. An Eastern European immigrant friend of mine once related to me the following experience. He was riding in an elevated train with his six-year-old son. The youngster continued to ignore his cautions against standing close to the entrance. He cuffed the boy a few times. Thereupon another passenger arose, advanced menacingly and said angrily: "If you dare to strike that child again I'll have you arrested."

The extent to which some American parents go to suit the convenience of their children is exemplified by a mid-Western couple I know. To make their little ones happy, they installed a fancy slide in their living room. Guests entered the apartment by bending under it, and then they attempted to enjoy a conversation within reach of the boisterous sideshow provided by the young ones going up and down.

That this is unusual even for the United States is indicated by the fact that this couple felt compelled to justify their action every time they had a visitor and by the fact that their friends remarked about it. On the other hand, no Chinese parents could have kept the respect of the community if they permitted anything remotely resembling this.

For many centuries Chinese were both entertained and instructed by some tales known as "The Twenty-Four Examples of Filial Piety." These stories were illustrated in paintings, dramatized on the stage, recited by story-tellers in tea houses and in market places all over the country. Here is one of these "examples":

A poor man by the name of Kuo and his wife were confronted with a serious problem. His aged mother was sick in bed. She needed both medicine and nourishment which Kuo could ill afford. After consultation between themselves, Kuo and his wife decided that the only way out was to get rid of their three-year-old only son. For Kuo and his wife said to each other, "We have only one mother, but we can always get another child." Thereupon the two went out to the field to dig a pit for the purpose of burying their child alive. But shortly after the man had started to dig he suddenly struck gold. It transpired that the gods were moved by the spirit of their filial piety, and this was their reward. Both the child and the mother were amply provided for and the family thrived happily ever after.

To the Chinese this story dramatized their most important cultural ideal, that support of the parents tops all other obligations and that this obligation must be fulfilled even at the expense of the children.

Economic support is not, however, the only way in which Chinese children are obligated to their parents. Their social duty toward their parents is even more striking. The son not only has to follow the Confucian dictum that "parents are always right," but at all times and in all circumstances he must try to satisfy their wishes and look after their safety. If the parents are indisposed, the son should spare no trouble in obtaining a cure for them. If a parent is sentenced to prison, the son must arrange to take that parent's place. If the parents are displeased with their daughter-in-law, the good son does not hesitate to think about divorce. In

the service of the elders, no effort is too extraordinary or too great.

Here again folktales are useful indications of the actual values. One classical story tells how a man gave up his hard-won official post in order to walk many miles in search of his long-lost mother. Another tells how a youngster of fourteen jumped on and strangled a tiger when the beast was about to devour his father. In a third story, a man cut a piece of flesh from his arm and boiled it in the pot with his father's medicine, believing that the soup would help the elder to recover from his long illness. Yet another tells us:

When the mother of the dutiful Wang Low was still alive in the days of the Wei dynasty, she was greatly afraid of thunder. After her death she was buried in a mountain forest. Whenever Low heard a thunderstorm he immediately ran to the graveyard, kneeled, and tearfully said: "Low is here, Mother, do not be afraid."

Moreover, many Chinese stories did not remain mere literature but were sometimes copied to the letter by over-filial sons. In the thousands of volumes of district histories and genealogical records to be found in every part of the country are many individual biographies of local greats. After a cursory reading of about fifty of them, I found at least five instances in which men and women were said to have sliced flesh from their arms to be boiled in the medicine pot of one or another of their parents. One man did this twice during one of his father's illnesses. Because the elder's condition remained serious, the filial son decided to take a more drastic course of action. He cut out a piece of what he thought was his "liver" instead. Both he and his father died shortly afterwards. Hundreds of other biographies contain less dramatic episodes, but all are variations on the same theme.

It is not suggested that all Chinese youngsters are indoctrinated in filial piety on the day of their birth, or that more than a handful of American parents have ever had occasion to be rebuked by strangers for the way they handled their own children. It is important to realize, however, that incidents and lore like the ones given are symptomatic of the different social climates in which parents and children in the two countries react to one another.

Given the American type of atmosphere, parents do not only wish to help their children according to the parents' experiences. They must try to find out by elaborate research what the youngsters really want, so that the elders can better satisfy the youngsters' individual predilections. Although it is true that children all over the world are inclined to play, American parents do not stop at giving their children every conceivable kind of toy. They feel compelled to reduce even the rudiments of a child's education to a matter of fun. Recently I came across two books advertised as *Playbooks That Teach Your Child to Dress,* one for boys and one for girls.

The toy industry of America rose from an annual business of a mere $150,000,-000 in 1939 to $750,000,000 in 1951. We may expect that this figure will increase in the next decade because of the increasing number of commercially profitable events such as local "baby weeks," the acceleration of learning by playing, and the coming and going of fashions in playthings as in other products. The annual business catering to all infant needs has reached, in 1951, an astronomical $5,000,-000,000. Television today, as has radio for years, has scores of programs designed for children. Their announcers advise the kiddies to tell parents that they will eat nothing but "Snapcrackles" for breakfast. The children do so, and most parents obey by purchasing the desired product.

The relations of Chinese parents and children exhibit none of these tendencies. Chinese parents are amused by infantile behavior and youthful exuberance, but the measure of their children's worth is determined primarily by the degree to which they act like adults. The sooner they do so the better. Chinese parents are rather proud of a child who acts "older than his age" where American parents are likely to take a similar child to a specialist. Or Chinese parents are apt to be upset by certain aspects of a child's behavior which would bring joy to American parents.

Take toys again for an example. Chinese children occasionally receive a toy. When I was six years of age my mother bought me a cart made of tinfoil. Soldered above the entrance to the cart was an ornamental rectangle. Having seen movable curtains on real carts, I attempted to lower the curtain at the entrance of my toy cart and yanked the stationary ornament out of place. An American mother would have gloated over the creative impulse of her "budding genius"; but my mother was very much displeased because she thought me destructive and temperamental. Had I acted the model child that the Chinese mother hoped for, by nursing one old toy for a couple of years, an American mother might have worried about the retarded or warped state of my mind.

The specific mechanisms through which Chinese and American children begin their contrasting ways of life are many. To begin with, the average size of the Chinese family is, contrary to popular belief, about five persons. The average number in an American family is three. More important than size is the fact that when an American speaks of a family he refers to a group composed of parents and unmarried children, whereas the Chinese term for family includes grandparents and in-laws. Even if Chinese grandparents and in-laws do not live under the same roof, they usually reside in the same village, a neighboring village, or at the farthest a neighboring district. On the other hand, Americans related by blood or legal bonds usually live so far from one another that this broader group does not come together except on such occasions as Easter, Thanksgiving, Christmas, or other holidays.

These differences mark the point of departure in the early experiences of Chinese and American children. The Chinese child grows up amidst continuing or frequent contacts with a number of related individuals besides his own parents and siblings, but his American counterpart grows up in much greater physical isolation. Very early in life the former is conditioned to appreciate the importance of getting along with a wide circle of relatives while the latter is not.

Far more crucial, however, is the manner of interaction between the growing child and individuals other than those making up his immediate family. American parents are the sole agents of control over their children until the latter are of age. The grandparents and in-laws do not ordinarily occupy a disciplinary role, whether they live in the same house or not. Even when grandparents take over during an emergency such as sickness or childbirth, the older people are supposed to do no more than administer things according to the laws laid down by the younger couple, more likely by the younger woman. The usual response of an American elder to any request made by his or her little grandchild is, "Does

your mother want you to?" When control is exercised over an American child, it is the parental arm that does so, no other.

Chinese parents have much less exclusive control over their children. In cases where grandparents do not share the same roof with them, during a brief visit the older couple can do almost anything that they see fit in regard to the children, even if it means going over the parents' heads. The liberty taken by most Chinese aunts, uncles, and in-laws might break up most American families. Furthermore, while an American mother exhibits her displeasure with an over-indulgent grandmother and is considered right by others, a Chinese mother doing the same thing is an object of censure rather than sympathy. The strength of the Chinese parental authority, far from being overpowering, usually varies with circumstances.

The inevitable result of the omnipresent and exclusive control of American parents over their children is greater and deeper emotional involvement. Since parents are all-powerful, their images in the mind of the growing child naturally are elevated above all else. To the extent that they are the only objects of worship, they also are liable to become the only oppressors. Accordingly, when an American likes his parents, they are his idols. When he dislikes them, they are his enemies. A conscious or unconscious attachment to one parent at the expense of the other, a situation which gave Freud ground for postulating his famed Oedipus complex, is the extreme expression of this situation.

Not knowing the American kind of close and exclusive relationship, the mutual affection of Chinese parents and children is toned down. Since parental authority varies with circumstances, the parental image in the mind of the growing child must necessarily share the spotlight with men and women held in much higher esteem, such as grandparents, and with those regarded as the equals of the parents, such as uncles and aunts. The feeling toward parents being divided and diluted, the child does not develop a paralyzing attachment to, or strong repulsion against, the elders. There is still less reason for the emergence of the Oedipal triangle, in which the child is allied to one parent against the other. Consequently, when the Chinese child likes his parents he fails to raise them to high heaven; when he dislikes them he still vents his displeasure with great reserve.

Contrary to popular belief, it is a fact that Chinese parents, though much more respected, revered, or even feared by their children than are American parents by theirs, actually leave much less of an impression on the character of their progeny, since the parent-child relationship is neither so close nor so emotionally charged.

The beginnings of the contrasts between the two ways of life now become apparent. In the American scene the child soon learns to follow his own predilections. For his environment is sensitive to *him*. In the Chinese scene the child soon learns to appreciate the importance of changing circumstances. For he is obliged to be sensitive to his *environment*.

Similarly, the American child tends to develop strong feelings of love or hate. For the exclusive parent-child bond inevitably concentrates emotions at a few points. The Chinese child tends to moderate his feelings in general. For his diffused relationship with parents and relatives likewise tempers his emotional involvements.

As Chinese and American children grow older the contrast between their experiences is intensified. American parents encourage their children to do things for themselves. At the age of three or four, American children are exhorted to be big boys and girls, to dress themselves, feed themselves, and defend themselves against bullies.

Chinese parents are pleased if their children can do any of these or similar things. They do not, however, make a point of encouraging them or bragging about them. As to defending themselves, the characteristic advice to Chinese children is "don't get into trouble outside, and run home if there is danger."

Yet, though consciously encouraging their children to grow up in some ways, American parents firmly refuse to let the youngsters enter the real world of the adults. For one thing, they leave their children with sitters when they go to parties. If they entertain at home they put the youngsters to bed before the guests arrive. Children have no part in parents' social activities.

Chinese parents take their children with them not only to wedding feasts, funeral breakfasts, and religious celebrations, but also to purely social or business gatherings. A father in business thinks nothing of bringing his boy of six or seven to an executives' conference.

This pattern is still adhered to by the majority of second, third and fourth generation Chinese-Americans in Hawaii. Like their Caucasian neighbors, Chinese organizers in Hawaii also resort to "family picnics" and "family evenings" and even athletics for the purpose of maintaining or increasing club or church enrollment. But, unlike their Caucasian neighbors, Chinese parents in Hawaii take their very young children with them on many more occasions, for example on social and business visits which regularly last until late at night.

The result is that while Chinese youngsters unobtrusively enter into the world of the adults, American youngsters tend to develop a world of their own. This is further accentuated by the Chinese parents' insistence on complete community of interests with children, as much as by the American parents' insistence on privacy for all individuals.

The business of American parents, social and commercial, is their private reserve, and no trespassing by children is allowed except on those rare and eventful occasions when an explicit invitation is extended. Newspaper "psychologists" frequently advise that a well-adjusted personality will result if parents do not burden their children with adult difficulties. By the same token, parents are also supposed to refrain from entering into the doings of their youngsters. These same advisors admonish worried mothers to disappear when their teen-age daughters entertain at home.

Not so among the Chinese. Chinese children consider it a matter of course to witness or even participate in adult negotiations, exactly as Chinese adults think nothing about joining in their children's activities. This reciprocity goes so far that neither has any qualms about opening letters addressed to the other.

Nothing is more strikingly symbolic of these profound differences than the fact that American children celebrate their birthdays among themselves, their parents being assistants or servants, while Chinese children's birthdays are occasions for adult celebration, in which children may be present, like in wedding or funeral feasts, but they are certainly not the center of attraction.

The line of demarcation between the adult and the child worlds is drawn in many other ways. For instance, many American parents may be totally divorced from the church, or entertain grave doubts about the existence of God, but they send their children to Sunday schools and help them to pray. American parents struggle in a world of tough competition where sheer cunning and falsehood are often rewarded and respected, but they feed their children with nursery tales in which the morally good is pitted against the bad, and in the end the good is invariably rewarded and the bad inevitably punished. When American parents are in serious domestic trouble, they maintain a front of sweetness and light before their children. Even if American parents suffer a major business catastrophe, they feel obliged to turn their tearful eyes to their children and fake a smile, saying, "Honey, everything is all right." This American desire to maintain the children's world separate from that of the adults is exemplified also by the practice of delaying transmission of the news to children when their parents have been killed in an accident, or concealing the facts from them when one of the parents goes to jail. Thus, in summary, American parents face a world of reality while their children live in the near ideal realm of the fairy tales where the rules of the parental world do not apply, are watered down, or are even reversed.

Chinese children, however, share the same world with their parents. While there is not complete accord between what Chinese parents teach and what they do, for all human beings are prone to leave some gap between the lesson and the deed, parents make little effort to hide their problems and real selves from their children. In triumph the children celebrate with the adults; in disaster the little ones suffer with them. Very early in life Chinese children learn that reward and punishment are not necessarily consistent with the established rules of conduct, and that justice and love do not always prevail. Yet at the same time they are more likely than American children to become conscious of the power exercised by the environment. For theirs is an environment that is very exposed, and young eyes without blinkers see their parents' faults as well as their virtues. From the beginning they see their parents not as giants astride the earth, moving mountains and slaying dragons, which is the American child's Bunyanesque interpretation of the scene, but as ordinary mortals succeeding at times but failing at others, following inevitably the paths marked by custom and tradition.

Thus the American child is not only increasingly convinced of the importance of his individual predilections, he is equally sure that no eventuality can deter him, the invincible individual, from realizing them in thought or action. In his restricted and comforting world he has experienced few irreparable setbacks and known few situations in which he is entirely frustrated by reality. Just as joy and good proceed from the parents, who focus upon themselves all attention and draw to themselves all power, it is they alone who can impose restrictions that the child may see as barriers to his own advancement.

The Chinese child is not only fully aware that he should obey his parents and other seniors, but even when he succeeds in circumventing them he still faces the hurdles presented by custom and tradition. Through his active observation of and participation in adult activities, he is already well versed, by hard knocks on the head, in his own shortcomings and the real nature of his society. The foci of attention and power being many, the restrictions imposed upon the individual come not from the parents, but the society at large. Even if he resents these barriers he can still see no point at which to center his attack, for they are too numerous and too diffuse.

Seymour Martin Lipset: THE UNCHANGING AMERICAN CHARACTER

Sociologists usually conclude that today's American differs markedly from his forebears; historians tend to search earnestly for continuities with the past. Seymour Lipset, currently at Harvard University, is an historically-minded sociologist. In one of the most important recent analyses of the American character he finds a continuity in the American value system — a system which has always placed a premium on the virtues of individual achievement and on equality. These two values, he claims, have been reshaped by various technological and economic changes through time, but they have persisted. In proposing his own version of the American character, Lipset not only looks back at most of the readings in this collection, but he also opens up many new areas of inquiry and many new questions of relevance in the continuing quest to understand what is American about Americans.

TWO THEMES, equality and achievement, emerged from the interplay between the Puritan tradition and the Revolutionary ethos in the early formation of America's institutions. In this section the thesis is advanced that the dynamic interaction of these two predominant values has been a constant element in determining American institutions and behavior. As we have seen, equalitarianism was an explicit part of the revolt against the traditions of the Old World, while an emphasis upon success and hard work had long been a part of the Protestant ethic. In addition, the need to maximize talent in the new nation's search to "overtake" the Old World placed an added premium on an individual's achievement, regardless of his social station. The relatively few changes that Andrew Jackson made in the civil service, despite his aggressive equalitarian ethos, and the fact that his appointments were well-trained, highly educated men, show that ability was valued along with equality in the young republic.

The relationship between these themes of equality and success has been complex. On the one hand, the ideal of equal opportunity institutionalized the notion that success should be the goal of *all*, without reference to accidents of birth or class or color. On the other hand, in actual operation these two dominant values resulted in considerable conflict. While everyone was supposed to succeed, obviously certain persons were able to achieve greater success than others. The wealth of the nation was never distributed as equally as the political franchise. The tendency for the ideal of achievement to undermine the fact of equality, and to bring about a society with a distinct class

character, has been checked by the recurrent victories of the forces of equality in the political order. Much of our political history, as Tocqueville noted, can be interpreted in terms of a struggle between proponents of democratic equality and would-be aristocracies of birth or wealth.

In recent years, many social analysts have sought to show how the increasing industrialization, urbanization, and bureaucratization of American society have modified the values of equality and achievement. In both the 1930's and the 1950's American social scientists were certain that the country was undergoing major structural changes. In the 1930's they were sure that these changes were making status lines more rigid, that there was a movement away from achieved status back to ascribed status, and that the equalitarian ethic was threatened as a consequence. Such typical writers of the 1950's as David Riesman and William H. Whyte contend that it is the achievement motive and the Protestant ethic of hard work that are dying: they think that the new society prefers security, emotional stability, and "getting along with others." Riesman posits a transformation of the American character structure from "inner direction" (i.e., responding to a fixed internal code of morality) to "other direction" (i.e., responding to demands of others in complex situations). Whyte believes that values themselves have changed. He argues that the old value system of the Protestant ethic, which he defines as the "pursuit of individual salvation through hard work, thrift, and competitive struggle," is being replaced by the "social ethic," whose basic tenets are a "belief in the group as

From *The First New Nation*, pp. 101–127, 137–139, © 1963 by Seymour Martin Lipset, Basic Books, Inc., Publishers, New York. Reprinted by permission of Basic Books, Inc., Publishers, and of Heinemann Educational Books Ltd.

the source of creativity; a belief in 'belong-ingness' as the ultimate need of the individual; and a belief in the application of science to achieve the belongingness."

If the changes suggested by the critics of the 1930's or the 1950's were occurring in the drastic form indicated in their books, then America no longer could be said to possess the traits formed as a consequence of its origin as a new nation with a Protestant culture. As I read the historical record, however, it suggests that there is more continuity than change with respect to the main elements in the national value system. This does not mean that our society is basically static. Clearly, there have been great secular changes — industrialization, bureaucratization, and urbanization are real enough — and they have profoundly affected other aspects of the social structure. Many American sociologists have documented changes in work habits, leisure, personality, family patterns, and so forth. But this very concentration on the obvious social changes in a society that has spanned a continent in a century, that has moved from a predominantly rural culture as recently as 1870 to a metropolitan culture in the 1950's, has introduced a fundamental bias against looking at what has been relatively constant and unchanging.

Basic alterations of social character or values are rarely produced by change in the means of production, distribution, and exchange alone. Rather, as a society becomes more complex, its institutional arrangements make adjustments to new conditions within the framework of a dominant value system. In turn, the new institutional patterns may affect the socialization process which, from infancy upward, instills fundamental character traits. Through such a process, changes in the dominant value system develop

slowly — or not at all. There are constant efforts to fit the "new" technological world into the social patterns of the old, familiar world. . . .

In brief, I attempt in this section to present some of the evidence for my thesis that it is the basic value system, as solidified in the early days of the new nation, which can account for the kinds of changes that have taken place in the American character and in American institutions as these faced the need to adjust to the requirements of an urban, industrial, and bureaucratic society.

Marcus Cunliffe has remarked on the American tendency to assert that a wondrous opportunity has been ruined, "that a golden age has been tarnished, that the old ways have disappeared, or that they offer no useful guide to a newer generation." He points out that, American belief to the contrary, there has been surprising continuity in American history as compared with the histories of European nations. This American propensity to feel that the country is going through a major change at any "present time" is related to an almost "inherent American tendency to believe that one has been cut off decisively from the past as if by a physical barrier." Cunliffe attributes this tendency to three main elements:

First it is a consequence of the undeniable fact of continuous and rapid social change since the origins of settlement. This process has, understandably, revealed itself in regrets and neuroses as well as in pride and exuberance. Second, the tendency is rooted in the constant American determination to repudiate Europe — Europe equated with the Past, in contrast with America as the Future — and so to lose the Past altogether. Third, the tendency is a consequence of the American sense of a society which is uniquely free to choose its own destiny. The sense of mission, of dedication and of infinite possibility, in part a fact and in part an article of faith, has led to acute if temporary despairs, to suspicions of betrayal and the like, as well as to more positive and flamboyant results.

In a sense, Cunliffe's analysis shows how some of the values we have seen arising from America's revolutionary origins continue to be a part of its image of itself. And perhaps more important, his observation that there has been more continuity in American history than in European history suggests that the values around which American institutions are built have not changed abruptly. Others have pointed out that America is an example of a country where social change does not have to destroy the fabric of society, precisely because it is based upon an ideological commitment to change.

The thesis that the same basic values which arose in the American Revolution have shaped the society under changing geographical and economic conditions, has also been advanced by many historians. Thus Henry Nash Smith has sought to show how the rural frontier settlements established in the West on the Great Plains reflected not only the physical environment but also "the assumptions and aspirations of a whole society." He has argued that revisions in the Homestead Act, which would have permitted large farms and a more economical use of arid land, were opposed by the new settlers because they believed in the ideal of the family farm. Walt Rostow suggests there is a "classic American style [which] . . . emerged distinctively toward the end of the seventeenth century as the imperatives and opportunities of a wild but ample land began to assert themselves over various transplanted autocratic attitudes and institutions which proved inappropriate to the colonial scene . . . [and] came fully

to life . . . after the War of 1812." And he further contends that this style has not changed basically, since "the cast of American values and institutions and the tendency to adapt them by cumulative experiment rather than to change them radically has been progressively strengthened by the image of the gathering success of the American adventure." Commager, writing of America in general, has said: "Circumstances change profoundly, but the character of the American people has not changed greatly or the nature of the principles of conduct, public and private, to which they subscribe." Three books dealing with American values, by Daniel Boorstin, Louis Hartz, and Ralph Gabriel, have each in a different way, argued the effective continuity of the fundamental ideals of the society.

The conclusions of these historians are affirmed also in a "lexicographic analysis of alleged American characteristics, ideals, and principles" reported in a myriad of books and articles dealing with "the American way." American history was divided for the purposes of the study into four periods, "Pre-Civil War (to 1865), Civil War to World War (1866–1917), World War to Depression (1918–1929), and Depression to present (1930–1940)." For each period a list of traits alleged by observers was recorded, and "when the lists for each of the four time periods were compared, no important difference between the traits mentioned by modern observers and those writing in the earlier periods of American history was discovered." Among the traits mentioned in all four periods were: "Belief in equality of all as a fact and as a right" and "uniformity and conformity."

THE UNCHANGING AMERICAN CHARACTER

Foreign travelers' accounts of American life, manners, and character traits constitute a body of evidence with which to test the thesis that the American character has been transformed during the past century and a half. Their observations provide us with a kind of comparative mirror in which we can look at ourselves over time. It is important to note, therefore, that the type of behavior which Riesman and Whyte regard as distinctly modern, as reflecting the decline of the Protestant Ethic, was repeatedly reported by many of the nineteenth-century travelers as a peculiarly American trait in their day. Thus the English writer Harriet Martineau at times might be paraphrasing *The Lonely Crowd* in her description of the American of the 1830's:

[Americans] may travel over the world, and find no society but their own which will submit to the restraint of perpetual caution, and reference to the opinions of others. They may travel over the whole world, and find no country but their own where the very children beware of getting into scrapes, and talk of the effect of actions upon people's minds; where the youth of society determine in silence what opinions they shall bring forward, and what avow only in the family circle; where women write miserable letters, almost universally, because it is a settled matter that it is unsafe to commit oneself on paper; and where elderly people seem to lack almost universally that faith in principles which inspires a free expression of them at any time, and under all circumstances. . . .

There is fear of vulgarity, fear of responsibility; and above all, fear of singularity. . . . There is something little short of disgusting to the stranger who has been unused to witness such want of social confidence, in the caution which presents probably the strongest aspect of selfishness that he has ever seen. The Americans of the northern states are, from education and habit, as accustomed to the caution of which I speak, as to be unaware of its extent and singularity. . . .

Few persons [Americans] really doubt this when the plain case is set down before them. They agree to it in church on Sundays, and in conversation by the fireside: and the reason why they are so backward as they are to act upon it in the world, is that habit and education are too strong for them. They have worn their chains so long that they feel them less than might be supposed.

Harriet Martineau is only one observer of early American life, and not necessarily more reliable than others. But it is significant that her comments on American "other-directedness" and conformism do not flow, as do those of other nineteenth-century visitors who made comparable observations, from fear or dislike of democracy. Many upper-class visitors, such as Tocqueville or Ostrogorski, saw here a threat to genuine individuality and creativity in political and intellectual life, in that democracy and equalitarianism give the masses access to elites, so that the latter must be slaves to public opinion in order to survive. Harriet Martineau, as a left-wing English liberal, did not come to America with such fears or beliefs. She remained an ardent admirer of American democracy, even though she ultimately decided that "the worship of Opinion is, at this day, the established religion of the United States."

The most celebrated post-Civil War nineteenth-century English visitor to America, James Bryce, saw inherent in American society "self-distrust, a despondency, a disposition to fall into line, to acquiesce in the dominant opinion. . . ." This "tendency to acquiescence and submission" is not to be "confounded with the tyranny of the majority. . . . [It] does not imply any compulsion exerted by the majority," in the sense discussed by Tocqueville. Rather Bryce, like Harriet Martineau fifty years earlier, described what he felt to be a basic psychological trait of Americans, their "fatalism," which involved a "loss of resisting power, a diminished sense of personal responsibility, and of the duty to battle for one's own opinions. . . ."

Although Harriet Martineau and James Bryce stand out among nineteenth-century visitors in specifying that these other-directed traits were deeply rooted in the *personalities* of many Americans, the general *behaviors* that they and Tocqueville reported were mentioned by many other foreign travelers. For example, a summary of the writings of English travelers from 1785 to 1835 states that one important characteristic mentioned in a number of books "was the acute sensitiveness to opinion that the average American revealed." A German aristocrat, who became a devotee of American democracy and a citizen of the country, stated in the 1830's that "nothing can excite the contempt of an educated European more than the continual fears and apprehensions in which even the 'most enlightened citizens' of the United States seem to live with regard to their next neighbors, lest their actions, principles, opinions and beliefs should be condemned by their fellow creatures." An interpreter of nineteenth-century foreign opinion, John Graham Brooks, mentions various other writers who noted the unwillingness of Americans to be critical of each other. He quotes James Muirhead, the English editor of the *Baedeker* guide to the United States, as saying: "Americans invented the slang word 'kicker,' but so far as I could see their vocabulary is here miles ahead of their practice; they dream noble deeds, but do not do them; Englishmen 'kick' much better without having a name for it." Brooks suggested that it was the American "hesitation to face unpleasant facts rather than be disagreeable and pugnacious about them, after the genius of our English cousins, that calls out the criticism."

The observation that the early Americans were cautious and sensitive has been made not only by foreign visitors but also, at different times, by Americans — as in fact many of the foreign authors report. In 1898, the American writer John Jay Chapman echoed Tocqueville's dictum of seventy years before, that he knew "of no country in which there is so little independence of mind and real freedom of discussion as in America." Chapman saw the general caution and desire to please as the source of many of the ills of his day:

"Live and let live," says our genial prudence. Well enough, but mark the event. No one ever lost his social standing merely because of his offenses, but because of the talk about them. As free speech goes out the rascals come in.

Speech is a great part of social life, but not the whole of it. Dress, bearing, expression, betray a man, customs show character, all these various utterances mingle and merge into the general tone which is the voice of a national temperament; private motive is lost in it.

This tone penetrates and envelops everything in America. It is impossible to condemn it altogether. This desire to please, which has so much of the shopman's smile in it, graduates at one end of the scale into a general kindliness, into public benefactions, hospitals, and college foundations; at the other end it is seen melting into a desire to efface one's self rather than give offense, to hide rather than be noticed.

In Europe, the men in the pit at the theatre stand up between the acts, face the house, and examine the audience at leisure. The American dares not do this. He cannot stand the isolation, nor the publicity. The American in a horse car can give his seat to a lady, but dares not raise his voice while the conductor tramps over his toes.

Although these accounts by travelers and American essayists cannot be taken as conclusive proof of an unchanging American character, they do suggest that the hypothesis which sees the American character changing with respect to the traits "inner-" and "other-directedness" may be incorrect.

THE UNCHANGING AMERICAN VALUES
AND THEIR CONNECTION WITH
AMERICAN CHARACTER

The foreign travelers were also impressed by the American insistence on equality in social relations, and on achievement in one's career. Indeed, many perceived an intimate connection between the other-directed behavior they witnessed and the prevalence of these values, such that the behavior could not be understood without reference to them. An analysis of the writings of hundreds of British travelers in America before the Civil War reports: "Most prominent of the many impressions that Britons took back with them [between 1836 and 1860] was the aggressive egalitarianism of the people." If one studies the writings of such celebrated European visitors as Harriet Martineau, the Trollopes (both mother and son), Tocqueville, or James Bryce, it is easy to find many observations documenting this point.

Baedeker's advice to any European planning to visit the United States in the late nineteenth or early twentieth century was that he "should, from the outset, reconcile himself to the absence of deference, or servility, on the part of those he considers his social inferiors." A detailed examination of the comments of European visitors from 1890 to 1910 reports general agreement concerning the depth and character of American equalitarianism:

Whether they liked what they saw or not, most foreign observers did not doubt that America was a democratic society. . . . Different occupations of course, brought differences in prestige, but neither the occupation nor the prestige implied any fundamental difference in the value of individuals. . . . The similarity of conclusions based on diverse observations was simply another indication of the absence of sharp class differences. Even hostile visitors confirmed this judgment. . . . Some foreign observers found the arrogance of American workers intolerable.

Even today this contrast between Europe and America with respect to patterns of equality in interpersonal relations among men of different social positions is striking. A comparison of writings of European visitors at the turn of this century with those made by British groups visiting here to study American industrial methods since World War II states that "the foreign descriptions of . . . America in 1890 and 1950 are remarkably similar. . . . The British teams [in the 1950's reported] . . . the same values . . . which impressed visitors a half century ago. Like them they found the American worker is more nearly the equal of other members of society than the European, with respect not only to his material prosperity, but also to . . . the attitudes of others toward him." And this attitude is apparent at other levels of American society as well. As one commentator put it when describing the high-status Europeans who have come to America in recent years as political refugees from Nazism and Communism:

With his deep sense of class and status, integration in American society is not easy for the émigré. The skilled engineer or physician who . . . finally establishes himself in his profession, discovers that he does not enjoy the same exalted status that he would have had in the old country. I met several young Croatian doctors in the Los Angeles area who were earning $25,000 to $35,000 a year, but still felt declassed.

American emphasis on equalitarianism as a dominant value is significant in determining what to many of the Europeans were three closely related processes: competition, status uncertainty, and conformity. Tocqueville, for example, argued that equalitarianism maximizes competition among the members of a society. But if equalitarianism fosters competition for status, the combination of the two values of equality and achievement results, according to many of the travelers, in an amorphous social structure in which individuals are uncertain about their social position. In fact, those travelers who were so impressed with the pervasive equalitarianism of American society also suggested that, *precisely as a result of the emphasis on equality and opportunity,* Americans were *more* status-conscious than those who lived in the more aristocratic societies of Europe. They believed, for example, that it was easier for the *nouveaux riches* to be accepted in European high society than in American. British travelers before the Civil War noted that Americans seemed to love titles more than Englishmen. European observers, from Harriet Martineau and Frances Trollope in the 1830's to James Bryce in the 1880's and Denis Brogan in recent years, have pointed out that the actual strength of equality as a dominant American value — with the consequent lack of any well-defined deference structure linked to a legitimate aristocratic tradition where the propriety of social rankings is unquestioned — forces Americans to *emphasize* status background and symbolism. As Brogan has remarked, the American value system has formed "a society which, despite all efforts of school, advertising, clubs and the rest, makes the creation of effective social barriers difficult and their maintenance a perpetually repeated task. American social fences have to be continually repaired; in England they are like wild hedges, they grow if left alone."

Status-striving and the resultant conformism have not been limited solely, or even primarily, to the more well-to-do classes in American society. Many of the early nineteenth-century travelers commented on the extent to which workers attempted to imitate middle-class styles of life. Smuts notes that visitors at the turn of this century were struck by "what they regarded as the spend-thrift pattern of the American worker's life"; Paul Bourget, a French observer, interpreted this behavior as reflecting "the profound feeling of equality [in America which] urges them to make a show." As Werner Sombart, the German sociologist and economist, put it, "since all are seeking success . . . everyone is forced into a struggle to beat every other individual; and a steeple-chase begins . . . that differs from all other races in that the goal is not fixed but constantly moves even further away from the runners." And in an equalitarian democracy "the universal striving for success [becomes a major cause of] . . . the worker's extravagance, for, as Münsterberg [a German psychologist] pointed out, the ability to spend was the only public sign of success at earning." And lest it be thought that such concerns with conspicuous consumption emerged only in the Gilded Age of the 1890's as analyzed by Veblen, sixty years earlier a medical study of the "Influence of Trades, Professions, and Occupations, in the United States, in the Production of Disease," described and analyzed behavior in much the same terms:

The population of the United States is beyond that of other countries an anxious one. All classes are either striving after wealth, or endeavoring to keep up its appearance. From the principle of imitation which is implanted in all of us, sharpened perhaps by the existing equality of conditions, the poor follow as closely as they are able the habits and manner of living of the rich. . . . From these causes, and perhaps from the nature of our political institutions, and the effects arising from them, we are an anxious, care-worn people.

While some Europeans explained American behavior that they found strange — the sensitivity, kindliness, concern for others' feelings, and moral meekness — by reference to the nature of political democracy or the overbearing desire to make money, others saw these traits as consequences of the extreme emphasis on equality of opportunity, the basic American value which they properly regarded as unique. Many argued that this very emphasis on equality, and the constant challenging of any pretensions to permanent high status, has made Americans in all social positions extremely sensitive to the opinions of others, and causes status aspirants greater anxiety about the behavior and characteristics indicative of rank than is the case with their counterparts in more aristocratic societies. Discussing the writings of various travelers, John Graham Brooks states:

One deeper reason why the English are blunt and abrupt about their rights . . . is because class lines are more sharply drawn there. Within these limits, one is likely to develop the habit of demanding his dues. He insists on his prerogatives all the more because they are narrowly defined. When an English writer (Jowett) says, "We are not nearly so much afraid of one another as you are in the States," he expressed this truth. In a democ-

racy every one at least hopes to get on and up. This ascent depends not upon the favor of a class, but upon the good-will of the whole. This social whole has to be conciliated. It must be conciliated in both directions — at the top and at the bottom. To make one's self conspicuous and disagreeable, is to arouse enmities that block one's way.

One may find an elaboration of this causal analysis among many writers at different periods. Thus Max Weber, after a visit to America in the early 1900's noted the high degree of "submission to fashion in America, to a degree unknown in Germany" and explained it in terms of the lack of inherited class status. Seven decades earlier another German, Francis Grund, who saw in American equality and democracy the hope of the world, nevertheless also believed that the ambiguous class structure made status-striving tantamount to conformity. He presents both sides of the picture in the following items:

Society in America . . . is characterized by a spirit of exclusiveness and persecution unknown in any other country. Its gradations not being regulated according to rank and title, selfishness and conceit are its principal elements . . . What man is there in this city [New York] that dares to be independent, at the risk of being considered bad company? And who can venture to infringe upon a single rule of society?

This habit of conforming to each other's opinions, and the penalty set upon every transgression of that kind, are sufficient to prevent a man from wearing a coat cut in a different fashion, or a shirt collar no longer à la mode, or, in fact, to do, say, or appear anything which could render him unpopular among a certain set. In no other place, I believe, is there such a stress laid upon "saving appearances."

James Bryce, a half-century later, also linked conformity to the ambiguity of the status system, particularly as it affected the wealthy classes. He pointed out that it was precisely the emphasis on equality, and the absence of well-defined rules of deference, which made Americans so concerned with the behavior of others and seemingly more, rather than less, snobbish toward each other than were comparably placed Englishmen.

It may seem a paradox to observe that a millionaire has a better and easier social career open to him in England, than in America. . . . In America, if his private character be bad, if he be mean or openly immoral, or personally vulgar, or dishonest, the best society may keep its doors closed against him. In England great wealth, skillfully employed, will more readily force these doors to open. . . . The existence of a system of artificial rank enables a stamp to be given to base metal in Europe which cannot be given in a thoroughly republican country.

In comparing the reactions of Englishmen and Americans to criticism,. James Muirhead (the editor of the American *Baedeker*) stated that "the Briton's indifference to criticism is linked to the fact of caste, that it frankly and even brutally asserts the essential inequality of man. . . . Social adaptability is not his [the Briton's] foible. He accepts the conventionality of his class and wears it as an impenetrable armor."

A number of the foreign travelers, particularly those who visited America after the 1880's, were startled to find overt signs of anti-Semitism, such as placards barring Jews from upper-class resorts and social clubs which denied them membership. But this, too, could be perceived as a consequence of the fact that "the very absence of titular distinction often causes the lines to be more clearly

drawn; as Mr. Charles Dudley Warner says: 'Popular commingling in pleasure resorts is safe enough in aristocratic countries, but it will not answer in a republic.'" The most recent effort by a sociologist, Howard Brotz, to account for the greater concern about close contact with Jews in America than in England, also suggests that "in a democracy snobbishness can be far more vicious than in an aristocracy."

Lacking that natural confirmation of superiority which political authority alone can give, the rich and particularly the new rich, feel threatened by mere contact with their inferiors. . . . Nothing could be more fantastic than this to an English lord living in the country in the midst, not of other peers, but of his tenants. His position is such that he is at ease in the presence of members of the lower classes and in associating with them in recreation. . . . It is this "democratic" attitude which, in the first instance, makes for an openness to social relations with Jews. One cannot be declassed, so to speak, by play activities.

The intimate connection between other-directedness and equalitarian values perceived by these observers recalls the same connection noted by Plato in his theoretical analysis of democracy. In *The Republic* we find these words:

[In a democracy, the father] accustoms himself to become like his child and to fear his sons. . . . Metic [resident alien] is like citizen and citizen like metic, and stranger like both. . . . The schoolmaster fears and flatters his pupils. . . . The young act like their seniors, and compete with them in speech and action, while the old men condescend to the young and become triumphs of versatility and wit, imitating their juniors in order to avoid the appearance of being sour or despotic. . . . And the wonderful equality of law and . . . liberty prevails in the mutual relations of men and women . . . the main result of all these things, taken together, is that it makes the souls of the citizens so sensitive that they take offense and will not put up with the faintest suspicion of slavery [strong authority] that anyone may introduce.

Plato's analysis points up the main question to which this chapter is addressed: Are the conformity and the sensitivity to others — "other-directedness" — observed in the contemporary American character solely a function of the technology and social structure of a bureaucratic, industrialized, urban society, as Riesman and Whyte imply, or are they also to some considerable degree an expected consequence of a social system founded upon the values of equality and achievement? It seems that sociological theory, especially as expounded by Max Weber and Talcott Parsons, and much historical and comparative evidence, lend credence to the belief that the basic value system is at least a major, if not the pre-eminent, source of these traits.

As Plato noted, and as the foreign travelers testify, democratic man is deeply imbued with the desire to accommodate to others, which results in kindness and generosity in personal relations, and in a reluctance to offend. All books that are published are "exalted to the skies," teachers "admire their pupils," and flattery is general. The travelers also bear out Plato's remarks about the socialization of children in a democracy. It appears that equalitarian principles were applied to child-rearing early in the history of the republic. Early British opinions of American children have modern flavor:

The independence and maturity of American children furnished another surprise for the British visitor. Children ripened early. . . . But such precosity, some visitors feared, was too often achieved at the loss of parental

control. Combe claimed that discipline was lacking in the home, and children did what they pleased. Marryat corroborated this. . . . Children were not whipped here [as in England], but treated like rational beings.

Harriet Martineau's description of child-rearing in the America of Andrew Jackson sounds like a commentary on the progressive other-directed parent of the mid-twentieth century:

My [parent] friend observed that the only thing to be done [in child-rearing] is to avoid to the utmost the exercise of authority, and to make children friends from the very beginning. . . . They [the parents] do not lay aside their democratic principles in this relation, more than in others. . . . They watch and guard: they remove stumbling blocks: they manifest approbation and disapprobation: they express wishes, but, at the same time, study the wishes of their little people: they leave as much as possible to natural retribution: they impose no opinions, and quarrel with none: in short, they exercise the tenderest friendship without presuming upon it. . . . the children of Americans have the advantage of the best possible early discipline; that of activity and self-dependence.

What struck the democratic Miss Martineau as progressive was interpreted quite differently by Anthony Trollope, who visited this country in 1860: "I must protest that American babies are an unhappy race. They eat and drink as they please; they are never punished; they are never banished, snubbed, and kept in the background as children are kept with us." And forty years later, another English visitor, typical of the many who described American child-parent relations during a century and a half, tells us that nowhere else, as in America, "is the child so constantly in evidence; nowhere are his wishes so carefully consulted; nowhere is he allowed to make his mark so strongly on society. . . . The theory of the equality of man is rampant in the nursery. . . . You will actually hear an American mother say of a child of two or three years of age: 'I can't *induce* him to do this. . . .' "

If these reports from the middle and late nineteenth century are reminiscent of contemporary views, it is still more amazing to find, in a systematic summary of English travelers' opinion *in the last part of the eighteenth and early years of the nineteenth centuries,* that the emphasis on equality and democracy had *already* created the distinctive American child-oriented family which astonished the later visitors:

A close connection was made by the stranger between the republican form of government and the unlimited liberty which was allowed the younger generation. . . . They were rarely punished at home, and strict discipline was not tolerated in the schools. . . . It was feared that respect for elders or for any other form of authority would soon be eliminated from American life. . . . As he could not be punished in the school, he learned to regard his teacher as an inferior and to disregard all law and order.

Equality was thus perceived by many of the foreign travelers as affecting the socialization of the child not only within the family but in the school as well. The German psychologist Hugo Münsterberg joins the late-eighteenth-century visitors in complaining, over a century later in 1900, that "the feeling of equality will crop up where nature designed none, as for instance between youth and mature years. . . . Parents even make it a principle to implore and persuade their children, holding it to be a mistake to compel or punish them; and they believe that the schools should be conducted in the same spirit." Various visitors were struck

by the extent to which the schools did carry out this objective. The following description by an Englishman of schools in the New York area in 1833 sounds particularly modern:

The pupils are entirely independent of their teacher. No correction, no coercion, no manner of restraint is permitted to be used. . . . Parents also have as little control over their offspring at home, as the master has at school. . . . Corporal punishment has almost disappeared from American day-schools; and a teacher, who should now give recourse at such means of enforcing instruction, would meet with reprehension from the parents and perhaps retaliation from his scholars.

Tocqueville also found examples of the American's mistrust of authority "even in the schools," where he marveled that "the children in their games are wont to submit to rules which they have themselves established."

The educational policies which have become linked with the name of John Dewey and labeled "progressive education" actually began in a number of school systems around the country long before Dewey wrote on the subject: "To name but one example, the lower schools of St. Louis had adopted a system intended to develop spontaneously the inventive and intellectual faculties of the children by the use of games and with no formal teaching of ideas, no matter how practical."

THE INADEQUACY OF A MATERIALISTIC
INTERPRETATION OF CHANGE

Many of the foreign observers referred to above explained the other-directedness and status-seeking of Americans by the prevalence of the twin values of equality and achievement. Character and behavior were thus explained by values. They pointed out that the ethic of equality not only pervaded status relations but that it influenced the principal spheres of socialization, the family, and the school, as well.

Both Whyte's and Riesman's arguments, in contrast, explain character and values by reference to the supposed demands of a certain type of economy and its unique organization. The economy, in order to be productive, requires certain types of individuals, and requires that they hold certain values. In the final analysis, theirs is a purely materialistic interpretation of social phenomena and is open to the criticisms to which such interpretations are susceptible.

The inadequacy of such an explanation of change in values and social character is best demonstrated by comparative analysis. British and Swedish societies, for example, have for many decades possessed occupational structures similar to that of America. Britain, in fact, reached the stage of an advanced industrial society, thoroughly urbanized, where the majority of the population worked for big business or government, long before any other nation. The occupational profiles of Sweden, Germany, and the United States have been similar for decades. If the causal connection between technology and social character were direct, then the patterns described as typical of "other-direction" or "the organization man" should have occurred in Great Britain prior to their occurrence in the United States, and should now be found to predominate in other European nations. Yet "other-direction" and the "social ethic" appear to be pre-eminently American traits. In Europe, one sees the continued, even though declining, strength of deferential norms, enjoining conformity to class standards of behavior. Thus, comparative analysis strikingly

suggests that the derivation of social character almost exclusively from the traits associated with occupational or population profiles is invalid. So important an element in a social system as social character must be deeply affected by the dominant value system. For the value system is perhaps the most enduring part of what we think of as society, or a social system. Comparative history shows that nations may still present striking differences, even when their technological, demographic, or political patterns are similar. Thus it is necessary to work out the implications of the value system within a given material setting — while always observing, of course, the gradual, cumulative effect that technological change has upon values.

In attempting to determine how American values have been intertwined with the profound changes that have taken place in American society, it is not sufficient to point out that American values are peculiarly congenial to change. Although equality and achievement have reinforced each other over the course of American history, they have never been entirely compatible either. Many of the changes that have taken place in family structure, education, religion, and "culture," as America has become a "modern" society, have manifested themselves in a constant conflict between the democratic equalitarianism, proclaimed as a national ideal in the basic documents of the American Revolution, and the strong emphasis on competition, success, and the acquisition of status — the achievement orientation — which is also deeply embedded in our national value system.

Richard Hofstadter has urged the recurring pattern of value *conflict* and *continuity* in commenting on papers presented at a conference on changes in American society:

Culturally and anthropologically, human societies are cast in a great variety of molds, but once a society has been cast in its mold — Mr. Rostow is right that our mold as a nation was established by the early nineteenth century — the number of ways in which, short of dire calamity, it will alter its pattern are rather limited. I find it helpful also to point to another principle upon which Mr. Rostow has remarked — the frequency with which commentators find societies having certain paradox polarities in them. . . . We may find in this something functional; that is, *Societies have a need to find ways of checking their own tendencies. In these polarities there may be something of a clue to social systems.* . . .

Mr. Kluckhohn's report contains some evidence that we have already passed the peak of this shift about which I have been speaking. I find some additional evidence myself in the growing revolt of middle-class parents against those practices in our education that seem to sacrifice individualism and creativity for adjustment and group values. Granted the initial polarities of the success ethic, which is one of the molds in which our society is cast, this ethic must in some way give rise, sooner or later, to a reaction. . . . I do not think that we must be persuaded that our system of values has ceased to operate.

The analyses of American history and culture in the nineteenth and twentieth centuries, by both foreign and native interpreters, often differ according to whether they stress democracy and equality, or capitalism and achievement. Generally, conservatives have found fault with the decline of individuality and the pampering of children, and have seen both as manifestations of democracy and equality; while liberals have noted, with dismay, tendencies toward inequality and aristocracy, and have blamed them upon the growth of big business. These contrary political philosophies have also characterized the interpretation of Ameri-

can culture that predominates at any given period. Arthur Schlesinger, Sr., has even tried to measure the systematic characteristic duration of the "epochs of radicalism and conservatism [that] have followed each other in alternating order" in American history.

A cursory examination of the numerous differences between the conclusions of American social scientists in the 1930's and in the 1950's shows the way in which interpretations of American culture vary with social conditions. Writers of the 1930's amassed evidence of the decline of equalitarianism and the effect of this on a variety of institutions. Karen Horney in *The Neurotic Personality of Our Time*, for example, named anxiety over chances of economic success as the curse of what she, with many of her contemporaries, regarded as a completely pecuniary, achievement-oriented culture dominated by the giant corporations. Such analysts as Robert S. Lynd, and W. L. Warner all agreed that the egalitarian emphasis in American democracy was declining sharply under the growth of the large-scale corporation, monopoly capitalism, and economic competition. They asserted categorically that mobility had decreased, and Warner predicted the development of rigid status lines based on family background.

Twenty years later, these interpretations are almost unanimously rejected. Warner himself in one of his most recent works, shows that chances of rising into the top echelons of the largest corporations are *greater* than they were in the 1920's. As indicated earlier in this chapter, typical writers of the 1950's are concerned that the emphasis on achievement in American society may be dying out.

In large measure, the difference between writers of the two decades reflects the contrast between the economic circumstances of the times. The depression of the 1930's inclined intellectuals toward an equalitarian radicalism, which condemned capitalism and achievement orientation as the source of evils. Even a conservative like Warner was led to emphasize the growth of inequality and the restriction of opportunity. The prosperity of the 1950's, however, renewed the legitimacy of many conservative institutions and values, and discredited some of the innovations of the previous decades. The social analyses of the 1950's, even those written by men who still consider themselves liberals or socialists, involved at least a critique of the radical excesses of the former period, if not a critique of equalitarian values themselves. Perhaps the similarity in attitudes between the analysts of the 1950's and many of the foreign travelers of the last century is due to the fact that most of the European visitors have been conservatives, or members of the elite of much more aristocratic societies, and the modern Americans reflect the post-war revival of conservative values.

While Riesman and Whyte would deny that their works contain conservative value preferences, and insist that they are simply analyzing changes, it seems fairly evident that like the more elitist travelers of the nineteenth century, they deplore many of the dominant trends. They point to the spread of progressive education, with its disbelief in rewards for hard work, as illustrating the decay of the Protestant ethic, and they assume, as a result of this, a decline in the opportunity for developing creativity. Whyte points to the shift in scientific research from individual to group projects, which in his opinion are less creative. Neither Riesman nor Whyte explicitly asserts that there is more conformity now than in the past, for the

reason that men have always conformed to the values of the day; but both argue that contemporary values and personality traits emphasize accommodation to others, while the declining Protestant ethic and the inner-directed character structure stressed conformity to a fixed rule of conduct rather than to the fluctuating actions and moods of others.

This reaction against the apparent decline of the Protestant ethic of achievement and hard work, which has become a dominant theme among the intellectual middle class of the 1950's and early 1960's, should be viewed as the counterpart of the concern with the seeming breakdown of equality which moved comparable groups in the 1930's. The differences in the concerns of the two periods illustrate the important point that although the equalitarian ethos of the American Revolution and the achievement orientation of the Protestant ethic are mutually supporting, they also involve normative conflict. Complete commitment to equality involves rejecting some of the implications of valuing achievement; and the opposite is also true. Thus, when the equalitarianism of left or liberal politics is dominant, there is a reaction against achievement, and when the values of achievement prevail in a conservative political and economic atmosphere, men tend to depreciate some of the consequences of equality, such as the influence of popular taste on culture. . . .

Many analyses of American society have stressed the fact that individualism *and* conformism, creative innovation *and* dominance by low-level mass taste, are outgrowths of identical forces. For example, the pronounced spread of higher education and a high standard of living have caused an unprecedented increase in both the proportion of the population involved in genuinely creative, intellectual activities, and the influence by the populace on the major expressions of art, literature, and drama. Alexis de Tocqueville was fully aware of these dual tendencies when he pointed out that "the same equality that renders him [The American] independent of each of his fellow citizens, taken severally, exposes him alone and unprotected to the influence of the greater number. . . . I very clearly discern two tendencies; one leading the mind of every man to untried thoughts, the other prohibiting him from thinking at all."

Today, too, there are many trends making for an increase in autonomous behavior, in free choice. Various social scientists have recently begun to document these countervailing tendencies, a phenomenon that may reflect the ever-present cyclical pattern of social analysis. Rowland Berthoff points to the seeming "gradual decline since 1920 of those makeshift communities, the fraternal lodges," which were part of the associational pattern that impressed Tocqueville, and suggests that "the psychic energy that Americans formerly expended on maintaining the jerry-built framework of such 'institutions' as these has in our more assured institutional structure of recent years been freed, at least potentially, for the creation of more valuable kinds of 'culture.' " He also infers that "the recent popular success of books deploring the unworthiness of status striving indicates that Americans are throwing off this obsession and making it, as in other societies, including preindustrial America, merely one concern among many." Robert

Wood suggests, in the same vein, that "the pattern of inconspicuous consumption, the web of friendship, and the outgoing life that Whyte describes also have something of the flavor of a renaissance. Although 'keeping down with the Joneses' may indicate group tyranny, it is still better than keeping up with them. At least it displays disapproval of overt snobbishness. . . . While Whyte finds pressures for benevolent conformity, he also discovers brotherhood." Daniel Bell has argued that the growth in education, among other factors, has reduced conformity. He comments that "one would be hard put to find today the 'conformity' *Main Street* exacted of Carol Kennicott thirty years ago. With rising educational levels, more individuals are able to indulge a wider variety of interests," such as serious music, good books, high-level FM radio, and the like.

It may be fitting to conclude this chapter with the paradox formulated by Clyde Kluckhohn, who has suggested:

Today's kind of "conformity" may actually be a step toward more genuine individuality in the United States. "Conformity" is less of a personal and psychological problem — less tinged with anxiety and guilt. . . . If someone accepts outwardly the conventions of one's group, one may have greater psychic energy to develop and fulfill one's private potentialities as a unique person. I have encountered no substantial evidence that this "conformity" is thoroughgoingly "inward."

As status-seeking is the by-product of strong equalitarianism, so conformity and other-directedness may permit, or even demand, inner autonomy.

Suggestions for Further Reading

European travelers' accounts furnish one of the rich sources for commentary upon the American character. In addition to the writings of Crèvecœur, Tocqueville, Martineau, Dicey, Baron von Hübner, and Bryce, good sense is made by Michel Chevalier, *Society, Manners and Politics in the United States* (Boston, 1839); Charles Dickens, *American Notes* (New York, 1842); Fredrika Bremer, *America of the Fifties* (New York, 1853); J. F. Muirhead, *America, The Land of Contrasts* (Boston, 1898); Hugo Münsterberg, *American Traits from the Point of View of a German* (Boston, 1901); Philip Gibbs, *People of Destiny* (New York, 1920); and Denis W. Brogan, *The American Character* (New York, 1944).

These books must, however, be used with great care. When the foreigners spoke of the national character they were frequently careless with definitions and logic. The student should be aware of the pitfalls and potentialities in the use of the concept of national character. The best methodological introductions to this general problem include Margaret Mead, "The Study of National Character," in Daniel Lerner & Harold Lasswell, eds., *The Policy Sciences* (Stanford, 1951); Walter P. Metzger, "Generalization about National Character: An Analytical Essay," in Louis Gottschalk, ed., *Generalization in the Writing of History* (Chicago, 1963); Abram Kardiner, et. al., *The Psychological Frontiers of Society* (New York, 1945); and Reuel Denney, "How Americans See Themselves," in J. J. Kwiat & Mary C. Turpie, eds., *Studies in American Culture* (Minneapolis, 1960). Except for the Kardiner selection, these essays are quite short and not as foreboding as they may sound.

With or without method all kinds of writers have been tempted to delineate the American character. Among the more illustrious historians, Arthur M. Schlesinger Sr. has re-asked Crèvecœur's oft-repeated query in his chapter, " 'What Then Is the American, This New Man?' " in his *Paths to the Present* (New York, 1949). Henry Steele Commager compared the nineteenth-century American with his twentieth-century counterpart in the first and last chapters respectively of *The American Mind* (New Haven, 1950). David Potter has proceeded with somewhat more caution in his brilliant *People of Plenty* (Chicago, 1954). The first part probes the methodological problems of the study of national character and indicates how historians and behavioral scientists might benefit from each other's work. The second section studies the effect in many areas of American life of one very important factor — American abundance — in shaping the American character. He has also underlined a curious omission from American character studies in "American Women and the American Character," *Stetson University Bull.*, LXII (Jan., 1962), 1–22. The importance of mobility in shaping Americans has been recalled by George W. Pierson, "The M-Factor in American History," *Amer. Quar.*, XIV (Summer, 1962 Supplement), 275–289.

The nation's citizens have been psychoanalyzed in Geoffrey Gorer's eccentric study of *The American People* (New York, 1948) and in Erik Erikson's arresting "Reflections on the American Identity" in his *Childhood and Society* (New York, 1950). Gorer has added a postscript in his 1963 edition of *The American People* and Margaret Mead has done the same in her new 1965 edition of

And Keep Your Powder Dry: An Anthropologist Looks at America (New York, 1943). Other general studies of interest are Harold J. Laski, *The American Democracy* (New York, 1948); Ralph Barton Perry, *Characteristically American* (New York, 1949); Jacques Barzun, *God's Country and Mine* (New York, 1954); Louis Kronenberger, *Company Manners: A Cultural Inquiry into American Life* (New York, 1954); Max Lerner, *America as a Civilization* (New York, 1957); and Howard Mumford Jones, *O Strange New World: American Culture: The Formative Years* (New York, 1964).

The debate surrounding David Riesman's *The Lonely Crowd: A Study of the Changing American Character* (New Haven, 1950) has centered on the question of change and continuity in the American character. Riesman received support from William H. Whyte, Jr., who in *The Organization Man* (New York, 1956) spoke of the change from belief in the Protestant Ethic to the new faith in the so-called Social Ethic. A thorough and perceptive examination of this problem of change in American values may be found in Clyde Kluckhohn, "Have There Been Discernible Shifts in American Values During the Past Generation?" in Elting E. Morison, ed., *The American Style* (New York, 1958). *The American Style* also contains worthwhile pieces by Walt Rostow and Henry A. Murray. The most complete discussion of the pros and cons of *The Lonely Crowd* is S. M. Lipset and Leo Lowenthal, eds. *Culture and Social Character: The Work of David Riesman Reviewed* (Glencoe, Ill., 1961). Of special value in this collection are the essays by the two editors: Lowenthal's "Humanistic Perspectives of *The Lonely Crowd,*" and Lipset's "A Changing American Character?", the latter being

an earlier statement of the essay from *The First New Nation* which is reproduced above. The editors also give Riesman a chance at rebuttal in the last essay of the book; David Riesman and Nathan Glazer, "*The Lonely Crowd*: A Reconsideration in 1960." See also Carl N. Degler, "The Sociologist As Historian: Riesman's *The Lonely Crowd,*" *Amer. Quar.*, XV (Winter, 1963), 483–97 and Cushing Strout, "A Note on Degler, Riesman and Tocqueville," *Amer. Quar.*, XVI (Spring, 1964), 100–02. Degler finds all kinds of examples of other-direction in the nineteenth century while Strout chides Degler and other fellow-historians for ignoring real change in their single-minded search for continuity with the past —a pursuit peculiarly congenial to historians.

American "traits" form the subject of three challenging essays: Lee Coleman, "What Is American? A Study of Alleged Traits," *Social Forces*, XIX (May, 1941), 392–99; Maurice L. Farber, "English and Americans: A Study in National Character," *Jour. of Psychology*, XXXII (1951), 241–49; and Cora Du Bois, "The Dominant Value Profile of American Culture," *Amer. Anthropologist*, LVII (Dec. 1955), 232–39. Louis Hartz, Frederic Hoffman, David Potter, Paul Samuelson, and Leslie A. White gave papers at a University of Texas Symposium in 1962 on the subject of twentieth-century American individualism; Potter's was the best, but each presented many insights. They are all reprinted in "Individualism in Twentieth-Century America," *Texas Quar.*, VI (Summer, 1963), 97–176.

The most discerning and up-to-date bibliography on the general subject of the American character may be found at the end of Michael McGiffert's valuable book of readings, *The Character of Americans* (Homewood, Ill., 1964).